From Strive to Thrive

My journey with mental illness, addiction and God

GAYLE CHAPMAN

Cover illustration 'Alone' by Gayle Chapman, 2016.

Copyright © 2018 Gayle Chapman

gaylech@shaw.ca

All rights reserved.

ISBN-13:

978-1719438476

ISBN-10:

1719438471

Published in Victoria, British Columbia

DEDICATION

I dedicate this book to my friends Ann Maffey and Joan Smith who provided some funding to publish it; to Jody Paterson, who encouraged me to write it; to my sister Anne whose compassion and support gave me courage to fight for my life in my later years; and to Paul Willcocks, my editor, whose dedicated work has made this book a reality.
Also to all those who have faith in my story and seek to find out what makes me tick.

CONTENTS

	Introduction	1
1	An Unhappy Beginning	3
2	Home	8
3	Sunnier Memories	14
4	School	18
5	Life Changes	23
6	Beginning of Faith	26
7	Secrets	31
8	Unravelling	35
9	Flames	41
10	Forsaken	46
11	My Addictions	51
12	Hospitalized	55
13	Life With Betty	59
14	Dad Remarries	64
15	Lost In Addiction	69
16	I Become A Teacher	74
17	My Thirties: Lost Friends, Lost Years	77
18	Prison	83
19	Turning Forty In Jail	89
20	Free, Not Free	93
21	Reaching Out	99
22	Hospital And A New Home	105
23	Life On My Own	110
24	I Create A Program	116
25	My Walk With God	121
26	Neighbours And Near-Death	124
27	Empress Street And Art	132
28	Hayley Porteous	144
29	Rockland Apartments	147
30	God's Not Finished With Me Yet	159
	Acknowledgements	164
	About The Author	171

INTRODUCTION

I gazed at the television, horrified. My church, St. John the Divine, was engulfed in flames. I knew, with another huge, burdensome secret added to my cache, that this fire was my fault. It didn't matter that I hadn't set the fire. I felt the guilt.

Perhaps I was born with a mental illness. It was part of my family history. Or maybe I became ill during the tosses and turns of my childhood, and that carried on into my teen and adult life. I was diagnosed as an adult with bipolar and borderline personality disorders, and these two illnesses greatly influenced my decisions in life and led to the often negative outcomes.

My purpose in writing this book has been to reach younger people. Though you may not experience the same situations as I did, you might still experience overwhelming guilt, anger, shame, fear, self-loathing and self-harm. I want you to know that, in spite of all that life can throw at us, there is always an element of hope — even with a mental illness lapping at the door of our mind.

I dealt with my mental illness in a variety of ways. Most were harmful, and most of the people I sought help from became toxic to me. I wanted help to release the indescribable secrets that I carried, constantly piling higher and higher in my mind. Secrets I sought to forget through substance abuse and self-harm.

I never planned to live to my middle sixties. However, my struggles to find God in my life seemed to dictate a journey that would keep me from permanent harm.

This is not a self-help book. I'm sharing my journey. I'm writing about my experiences and know others might have perceived me differently during those tumultuous times. Feelings of abandonment left me searching in all the wrong places for peace and comfort.

What would you have done in these situations? My life, with mental illness and loss, took me into a tragic world. May you find solace in knowing that I really was not alone in my battles.

Now journey with me as I tell my story. I ask that you do not judge me or my predicaments. I had no understanding or awareness that I was plagued with mental illness, I just thought the world was contaminated and I needed to find a way to find peace in my life by coming to terms with my secrets.

This is my story.

1 AN UNHAPPY BEGINNING

I have always believed that my mom, on the morning of my birth, was ever so thankful to get me out of her system. I was a blue baby, born with too little oxygen in my blood. And at the moment of delivery, I somehow became both invisible and annoying at the same time.

I entered the world on Thanksgiving Day in Victoria, B.C., in 1950.

It was a stormy day — almost two inches of rain fell. Perhaps that's why I was named Gayle. Not the usual spelling for a windstorm, but whatever prompted my parents to choose the name, it had a ring to it that would clang throughout the rest of my life.

I wondered later in life whether my mother was pleased to see me even on that day. I know she hadn't been pleased to see my older sister, Joan, when she arrived three years and two days earlier. And I doubt she was happy to see my sister Anne who arrived about two and a half years after me. But whether she was happy about it or not, we became a family, with Eileen and John at the head. But not a happy one.

My mom was tormented, it seemed to me, by Joan's speedy arrival only thirteen months after their wedding day. Looking back as an adult, I have often felt that my mom felt cheated out of my dad's affections. Perhaps she moved away from an unhappy home through marriage. I am sure she expected to live a fairy tale life — love, commitment, and happy ever after. However, with the arrival of Joan, my mom's plans were torpedoed and her vision of the future sank into the angry abyss of lost dreams.

Mom had known my dad all her life as they grew up in neighbouring houses in Winnipeg. Being childhood playmates and then teen sweethearts, I think it seemed inevitable that they would marry someday. The Nixons — my mom's family — and the Chapmans lived next to each other. The mothers in both families, my grandmothers, had worked together in the post office when their children were young.

Though we never talked about my parents' courtship or wedding, a snapshot I saw from the wedding day still remains fixed in my mind. My mom, thin, sad-looking with downcast eyes, holding a small bouquet of flowers to enhance her simple wedding gown with its lace trim, stood stiffly across from my dad who, in his dark suit, looked debonair. His ever-present crooked smile and burning beady eyes spoke to me of a man who was looking for comfort and escape from his sorrow-filled youth. Both were tying the knot after the war ended — 1946. Their courtship and wedding were never talked about, and anyway, I wasn't interested in knowing the details of the wedding when I was young. I just presumed they married happily. I was more interested in surviving the constant fighting that must have begun shortly after they were married.

By the time I was born that Oct. 9, I think my mom saw me as another batch of cloth diapers to wash, another baby to bath, clothe and feed while her first was still a toddler and also needing a lot of attention.

My mom, tiny in stature, loved to wear house dresses and her slim figure modelled them well. In the 1950s the house dress was a symbol (at least to me) of the contented wife and mother. Her dark, tightly wavy hair complemented her wifely uniform and she had a rather sexy look about her. She moved quickly and precisely and often seemed high strung. Her demeanour exuded control. She meant business and was a whirlwind of activity.

Somehow I always had the impression, though, that my mom was just not up to such constant and demanding tasks. Even though she had a small and fragile frame, physically she could handle the chores and her children. However, I often imagined that she did not want to be a housewife and mother, or spend her days with her children hanging from the hem of her dress. Yet somehow she managed to keep us the best dressed, the best fed and the cleanest kids on our block. She was a perfectionist, and the strain of meeting her self-imposed standards must have taken a huge toll on her stamina, but, triumphantly, she did. Once Anne was born, my mother was looking after three children, the oldest just five, but that didn't stop her from setting high goals for herself, and for us.

The arrival of Anne, born when I was two, still did not deter my mother's high ideals for us all. Nor did it change the rhythm of life in the Chapman household or our world of secrets, shattered dreams, loneliness, bickering, jealousy and abuse.

I believe my mom disliked my older sister Joan almost from the moment of conception. Joan was not wanted, and we all knew that. Joan was so unwanted that the bickering over her must have begun as soon as my mother discovered she was pregnant.

My dad worked as a plumber, following the career he had apprenticed for in the navy. Unfortunately, in the 1950s plumbing was a somewhat seasonal trade. Much later in life I learned he hated plumbing and dreamed of being a carpenter. Dad was aggressive in his expectations of us, and my sisters and I seemed to have the unspoken task of meeting his needs for the love and affection that our mother refused him. He would force us to kiss and hug him, even when we cringed from these acts of forced comfort. He became Joan's protector, keeping her away from the anger and jealousies of my mom. This was not an easy or always successful undertaking, especially since my mom was constantly throwing my dad out of the house. He would be gone for unpredictable amounts of time before coming begging to let him back. Joan, as a result, was often undefended and left open to the wiles of my mom's hate.

Joan was helpless in the face of my mom's anger, and my mom never seemed to try to bond with her.

For most of my growing up years, the battles between my parents were over Joan — over the way my mom treated her and my dad's efforts to protect her — and later over Joan and money. Joan usually was at the centre of my mom's insecurities. Later in life, I realized my mom's need to be Number One in my dad's eyes was never fulfilled. Mom's constant rage with Joan was her response.

Once Anne and I arrived on the scene, we became targets for abuse as well. Uncontrolled yelling, free use of a leather strap, pushing, ego blasting, locking us in our rooms — our mom seemed always angry. These type of acts happened often — too often — particularly when my mom was in her angry, despondent, controlling moods. I cowered when her face turned dark grey and would often run and hide, quaking in my boots and crying.

Joan was wrongly punished on a regular basis. She was a bedwetter, thought to be the result of stress and fear over the emotional turmoil in the house, and my mother took great pleasure in humiliating her at any chance. It was not unusual for Joan to have to stay in her wet pajamas all day long, and she had to wash her sheets every day using the wringer washing machine.

One day, when I was about four and Joan about seven, I was sitting on the basement stairs watching Joan as she started wringing her bedsheets, as my mom worked nearby. Suddenly there was an ear-shattering scream as Joan's arm was caught between the wringers. I thought mom would rush over and release the two rollers and remove Joan's arm — but she didn't. She just walked away.

At that moment, I realized that I could never expect compassion from my mom and that I was not safe around her. From then on I avoided her and pushed her from my life, moving into my quickly developing dream world. She scared me — and I knew I was on my own to fend for myself.

My great aunt Mary and my uncle Charlie and their families lived in Victoria, but we had no other nearby relatives. In my teens my mom's mother came to live in Victoria, but there was so much tension between my grandmother and mother. My grandmother insatiably wanted attention, but would not accept it from my mom. I often felt I was the only one who got along with her, as I never remember my grandmother being mean to me.

However, my parents' main contact was with our godparents Maurie and Dot. Dot, who never had children, seemed to be a mentor to my mother. I loved Dot as she was funny and very kind. However, early in my life leukemia took her from us and we just had Maurie, who appalled me.

As I grew a little older, I began to realize I could not protect Joan from the criticism and turmoil and attacks. I felt so helpless from the moment I could comprehend what was going on in our home.

And I could not protect myself. When I was about five, I dropped a glass milk bottle on the floor while taking it from the refrigerator. It shattered, making a huge mess on the kitchen floor.

My mother screamed at me over and over again about the waste and the mess. She ran, livid, to the hall cupboard next to my bedroom, and yanked open the door. Without hesitating, she grasped a small, brown-striped suitcase and stomped into my bedroom. I could hear my bureau drawers opened and slammed shut. A few minutes later my mom returned to the kitchen, suitcase in hand. She shoved it at me and screamed "Get out. Go up to the orphanage. They will take you in. Do not come back."

I was terrified. I left crying and pleading for her not to send me away. Yet, there I was, clutching this little suitcase as I walked down Graham Street and turned right onto Kings Road, walking to the nearby B.C. Protestant Orphans' Home on the hill by the corner of Cook and Hillside. I dragged the suitcase up Kings Road, stopping once in a while to put the suitcase down and wipe my nose on my dress hem.

When I got there, I knocked on the massive door. I'd been there before. Children of the neighbourhood were always invited to share the orphans' Christmas parties. Mrs. Barnard was the matron who greeted us each year, and she answered the door this time as well. I explained, between sobs, that my mom had sent me there. "I was bad," I said. "I am to stay here."

Mrs. Barnard tried to console me. I suspect now that she phoned my mom, and then tried even harder to calm me down.

After a few hours, my dad arrived at the orphanage, looking quite embarrassed. Collecting me, he said nothing at all about mom's anger — he just took me back home.

Even now, I have great fears when leaving home. Though I no longer felt safe at home, leaving was even more terrifying.

Most of the time, I felt invisible to both my parents. The fighting over Joan was intensified by my mother favouring Anne, while my dad, always fighting to get my mom to ease up on Joan, favoured and protected Joan. I felt totally ignored, being in the middle of all fighting with no role. I was the favourite of neither parent. Often I would go to my room during these vicious melees and sit looking out the window, daydreaming of a far off, pleasantly quiet place, blocking out the screaming and the swearing. I never thought I was missed during these times and became used to being alone — though I never really wanted to be.

For a few years, I acted the clown to attract attention. I would be the funny one, break the tension and distract with a joke or a pun. But after a while I realized that my efforts were futile. I must have worked very hard at it; to this day I am the master of puns and odd jokes, especially when I am anxious or frightened. They were the first words and thoughts that seemed to make me unique.

But by the time I was five or six, these moments of hilarity ended, suffocated in the hostile space around me. I began to grow quiet and introverted. I knew even then that I was defeated, being relegated to a life of loneliness and despair.

I gave up. And when I did my mental health problems began. I was too young to recognize that my mother most likely suffered from bipolar disorder. I didn't know much about her deeply depressed mother and grandmother, neither of whom she got along with. Nor did I know much about my dad's mom, father and brother, who also suffered from mental health problems, My dad's father spent most of his life in an asylum outside Winnipeg.

My diagnosis was years away. But illness seized me, and I plunged into a crucible of torment and disregard for my own self-preservation.

2 HOME

A few days after I was born, we moved into the three-bedroom bungalow at 2537 Graham Street my parents had started building in 1947. Despite the three years of work, the basement and first floor weren't quite complete, but my parents decided with two children we needed more space, whether the house was ready or not. Up until the move, my parents and Joan were crammed into an apartment in a house on Green Street, not far from Graham. I am sure the trio were glad to have more space and more privacy when they moved.

The house was uniformly beige on the inside, with white stucco and pink trim on the outside — later, faux stonework was added to the front of the house, created with cement and crushed glass, a colour scheme that suggested femininity and peace. Little did the neighbours or those who passed by know that there was very little peace on the inside of that house.

The kitchen was my mother's empire. Red arborite counters, a red-topped chrome kitchen table and five chrome chairs upholstered in red vinyl. It was nothing fancy. However, it became the place where my mom could express her creativity. She loved to cook and bake, and spent hours and hours whipping up delights for us all. The kitchen was mom's realm of joy. Her happiest moments were when she was creating either a dinner or a cake. She often was not bothered by anyone as we respected her need for creativity and the chance to be alone. Our freezer, fridge and cellar were never empty, and, for the most part, we all appreciated her hobby.

The living room, which we were not allowed to enter except when guests came over, had an endearing fake fireplace, constructed of plaster with a wooden mantel, both also painted beige. In the fireplace was an electric fire that was only plugged in when company was visiting. The beige carpet matched the walls, and the chairs and couch, as was the norm in the '50s, were covered in plastic to preserve them. I can't even remember the colour of the first couch — just the plastic. But the living room was simply, yet elegantly, furnished with a coffee table, a couple of stately table lamps, three small but comfy chairs and venetian blinds over the window looking out onto the street. Only one picture hung on the wall — a Krieghoff print I believe — and it was over the couch which sat by the wall next to our dining room.

The dining room, where we entertained our godparents on Sunday evenings and where my parents played bridge with friends many Saturday evenings, was the hub of family entertaining. It was sparsely furnished with a wooden table and four chairs; three extra chairs were parked in the corners to accommodate extra guests. Many years later a china cabinet and hutch were added to the mix. Our most frequent company was our godparents. They came at least twice a month and we frequently dined at their place on Diamond Street. Theirs was a spacious 1950s home with lots of windows and doors and floors that we could slid across in our stocking feet. I will always remember the three black ceramic birds that hung on the wall over their kitchen table. Not only were they always there to magically greet me, but they never seemed dusty.

Sundays were special. We children had tea with our guests. My mom had a collection of demitasse cups just for the kids and, with a touch of milk, no sugar, the three of us imbibed with the older folks.

When tea was over we were sent to our rooms. All the bedrooms were off a semi-circular arched hallway — Anne and I, once she was old enough to share a room, in the southeast bedroom, Joan in the middle one, tucked behind the kitchen, and my parents on the southwest corner next to the living room. We prepared for bed. With PJs on, we were permitted to return to the living room with colouring books and crayons to begin our only calming Sunday night activity.

I loved colouring because I could access a very deep and private world within my soul and I did not have to share anything with anyone. I always had my own crayons and my own colouring books, so there was no need to interact with my sisters or fight over a colour. I was exceptionally good at colouring and this act of filling up spaces on a page always brought me peace. Every Christmas our godparents gave each of us a colouring book and a box of 64 Crayola crayons, and those were my most treasured gift — toys were not in abundance in those days.

But my mother forced me to stop colouring at 14, and the presents ended. Too childish, she told me. My world was totally shattered by this act and I didn't truly recover from this loss of personal identity for decades.

Our basement, which in essence was the "children's living room," was made up of many areas. In the southwest corner was a grotto where a 26-volume set of Columbia Encyclopedias sold to my parents by a door-to-door salesman, plus several annual 'updates,' shared space with a variety of adult and children's books. I read the entire set of encyclopedias in my childhood. There was a space for what toys we did own and a record player with many children's records. Music was my second vehicle into my private world. I loved classical music. When I was about nine or 10 my mother collected the most wonderful selection of classical records through a promotion at Safeway, just around the corner from where we lived. Each record came with a booklet describing the composer and the pieces of music, and I spent hours and hours studying them. With the final record purchase, a leather-bound binder was included and all the records and booklets were in one handy, but rather heavy, place. I would listen to these records for hours and hours, oblivious to time and what was happening in the world around me at home.

When I grew much older, a typing table with an old-fashioned manual typewriter and my music stand for practising the violin filled a space between the grotto and my mom's in-the-wall ironing board. The record player and the typewriter became the most important items in the basement in my early teens.

In the main part of the basement stood our black and white TV, surrounded by comfy, but not new, padded chairs and a pull-out couch. Later the floor was raised on 2x4s and covered with plywood and linoleum. But I remember watching television when the floor was just grey-painted cement, very cold on the feet, winter or summer.

Beside the basement living room was a space with a coal-burning furnace, a wood stove, the washing machine (a roller washing machine at first) and a double sink. Next to the laundry area was the coal room, filled through a chute that connected to the outside wall. Coal was delivered on a regular basis and often we kids would forget to shut the coal room door and black dust would fly all over the rest of the basement. Our forgetfulness was swiftly chastised. Later the coal furnace was replaced by an oil furnace, with an indoor tank. Eventually the coal room became my father's workshop and, years later, a photography lab.

My dad loved photography, or at least he let on that he did. It was not until he was dying that he let my sister Anne know that it was my mom's idea that he take it up — she wanted him to have a respectable hobby. I could never figure out why he rarely used the darkroom, but, after showing me how to develop and enlarge pictures, he left me to experiment. I loved spending these hours alone, closed off from the rest of the house, in a red-lighted world that seemed to have a curious effect on me. I felt powerful and never lonely.

Also in the basement, at the bottom of a second set of stairs from the kitchen, was a room where I spent hours and hours of my growing-up life inventing and creating. I was chuffed at making things like a puppet theatre out of a cardboard box, with puppets made from cutouts from a Simpson Sears catalogue. In my early teens, with great pride, I put together a microscope, something I had wanted desperately since I decided that I wanted to be a nurse when I grew up. My invention consisted of a toilet paper roll, a magnifying glass, a stick to hold the toilet paper roll and a block of wood to keep them all upright. I used and used my creation until, one Christmas a year or so later, I was given the real thing.

Often my sisters played with me, and we seemed to get along well in this space. With no parents to interfere with our basement life we flourished there.

Outdoors we had a real backyard with a vegetable garden, a grassy area for my sisters and I to play and a clothesline on which the weekly laundry would be hung to dry in any season. Later a garage was added at the north edge of the property, and my parents planted several small fruit trees and berry bushes next to a compost heap in the far corner. My mom loved gardening, especially flower gardening. As the years passed, our home was graced with many flower beds, full, mostly, of rose bushes. She would spend hours and hours spraying, pruning, digging, and just plain admiring her special crop.

As an adult I came to hate roses, probably out of spite of my mom, I would cringe in my later years whenever anyone gave me one. The memories of my mom were too powerful and too painful to remember and these roses always reminded me of what I wanted to forget. Eventually, though, I grew to love them. They were always given to me out of love and respect.

My sisters and I loved to play. Tag, hula hoop (made out of plastic pipe my dad used in his trade as a plumber), croquet, badminton, ball, jacks, plus many more games that kept us outdoors and busy for hours and hours, usually until the sun set. There was no sitting indoors watching TV (mainly because there was only one channel for years on the black and white).

Occasionally we had a friend over, though I must admit we did not have many of them. For many years the neighbourhood, though minutes from Victoria's downtown, was not developed. Most of the families lived down the hill from us and we rarely mingled with them. As the years rolled by more and more houses were built. But even though other families with children moved onto the street, I found friends were difficult to come by. Not one of us had soul-friends on the block and none of us ever brought other kids home from school. Somehow it was relayed to us that having other kids in the house was not allowed. With fear we kept this rule, but our loneliness and need for a kindred spirit were never really satisfied. My sisters were my companions, and we spent our days playing, and, frequently, fighting physically and verbally.

Nostalgia to me is really distorted memory. Past events and daily routines are viewed through a quainter lens, almost like looking through smog glass. I realize that my parents spent a lot of energy trying to convince the rest of the world that, as a family, we were peaceful, law-abiding citizens.

The reality was that behind the pink-trimmed front door we were secretly wrenched apart by violence, hate, anger, jealousies and physical abuse. My idyllic moments were surrounded with much loneliness and sadness. By age six, as the loneliness began to overwhelm me, negative behaviours began to surface.

My home life was uncomfortable and confusing, beyond a child's ability to comprehend. I now realize I was witnessing the destruction of my family as long periods of dysfunction and abuse were sprinkled with occasional good times. This marked our lives. From the outside, my early childhood perhaps seems relatively trauma free. But I now recognize that I, being very sensitive and easily hurt, believed I was one of the reasons the family seemed to be falling apart. I believed I needed to be punished for my role in this decline.

And I looked for any way to ease my anguish. Even as a young child, I searched the medicine cabinet in our bathroom for pills to swallow to numb these unpleasant feelings. By age eight, I began using my allowance to buy Aspirin and Contac C, taking massive doses of these as often as I could. I find it strange that I do not remember how I was able to continually buy my pills, especially since the pharmacy on the corner of Hillside and Quadra, where the Salvation Army building is now, was the only pharmacy in the area and it was a mom and pop business. Jerry, the pharmacist, knew all of us — I am quite sure he would have noticed large quantities of Contact C and Aspirin walking out of his store on a regular basis. My hunch is that I would leave our cozy little neighbourhood on my bike and buy supplies in other places around the city. In those days I was not afraid to go beyond our street.

By the age of six, I was beginning to consider suicide — in fact, when I was six I tried to hang myself in my bedroom cupboard with a belt I had stolen from my parents' bedroom. My mother discovered me hanging there while putting away the laundry. Angrily she pounced on me, unbuckled the belt, and screamed at me that she should take me to the police to deal with me. I was bad, bad, bad. This lack of caring led me to other suicide attempts.

My childhood, and the carefully crafted "idyllic life" my mother had tried to create for the world, had somehow poisoned me. And over the years I came to express that poisoning in terrifyingly negative acts towards myself.

3 SUNNIER MEMORIES

Sometimes I fear all that I write seems negative and, at times, almost unfair to my family and others. There were good times, but they came with their own perils.

Although I was severely depressed and suicidal, there were still moments where I experienced warm, fuzzy, tender and fun moments at home. These good times, unfortunately, seemed to revolve around my mother's "highs," which, I later realized, were her manic times. There were, in fact, wonderful moments that came with this state of her mind.

Most years, the time between August and mid-December, were full of pre-Christmas planning for my mom and, we caught the bug, my sisters and I, as well. The summer, with our yearly trip to the Okanagan Valley in British Columbia, was fruitful, to say the least. These trips were plotted out to see other sights as part of the journey — Barkerville, the Spiral Tunnel, Banff and Jasper parks and other such inspiring towns and landmarks — and to pick up the sweet, freshly picked fruit from the valley. Plums, peaches, pears, apples, cherries were among the fare that were arranged in little boxes in the trunk of our old Austin family car. My mom knew that the three of us would eat the fruity booty on the way home if left to our ways. So she always bought each of us a small box of mixed fruit to enjoy, knowing that when each of us had finished our cardboard carton of mixed fruit, we had filled our tummies with enough fruit to last us into fall.

When we arrived home from these trips, mom would immediately haul out the canner, the Mason jars, the lids, the paraffin wax, 10-pound bags of sugar and many jars of pectin and begin two weeks of almost around-the-clock work canning all that fruit. She had manic energy that seemed unstoppable. Quarts of this fruit and that fruit flew onto the shelves in the basement under our front porch stairs. While the rest of us, my dad included, slept, my mom hummed to the rhythm of the canner bubbling around the Mason jars. Sweating and tired, she would haul a kettle of sealed jars out of the canner and let them cool on a wooden sideboard next to the stove. I could tell she was in ecstasy throughout these days. I was so moved to see her happy. This state did not last, yet somehow throughout the next few months leading up to Christmas, her productivity and pleasure billowed.

From September until a couple of weeks before Christmas, baking was the order of the day — massive amounts of different varieties of cookies, Christmas cakes soaked in brandy and covered with linen, sweets like almond bark and succulent rainbow rolls. Each year the three of us would set about establishing a mother for ginger beer, a mix of raisins, lemon juice and zest, sugar, ginger and water. We would put a huge jar of this mixture on the radiator in the kitchen, adding more water each week, taking pride in the bubbling elixir that would be the base for batches of bottled ginger beer we brewed to be part of our Christmas fare. Eventually, a batch blew up all over the kitchen just around Christmas; after that, there was no more ginger beer brewed in our house. Yet, even then, there was so much joy within the walls of our home it was difficult not to be swept up by it.

As the freezer filled up and the days counted closer and closer to Christmas, the atmosphere started to change. Mom, tired I suspect from such an outpouring of energy, quieted down. The dark days of fall and winter seemed to bring on the darkness in her. My sisters and I barely really noticed the change; we were too busy checking out cupboards and suitcases for our stocking stuffers and presents, arguing among ourselves about who would get what. One year, my mom, getting wise to our yearly search, gave none of us any of the presents that we found earlier. The mystery remained and still remains — to whom did she give them?

In December, after we excitedly went to the Christmas tree lot near our house to pick out our tree, our dad's job was to put on the ancient, heavy long strings of lights. This seemed to take a whole afternoon of untangling, debating, and then attempting to put them on our tree. By evening we were ready to decorate. Mom supervised us, and the bickering between my dad and her slowly crept into the festivities. We were not immune to her criticisms and verbal jabs about not putting the decorations or tinsel on right, not arranging the presents or the stockings on the mantel to her satisfaction or leaving crumbs on the living room carpet as we snacked on some pre-Christmas cookies and sweets.

As Christmas day grew closer and closer, I hung out at church with the choir, frantically rehearsing the hymns and anthems for the midnight Christmas service. I loved Christmas at church, and in the Anglican church I was attending the music was magical and welcoming. The Saviour was heralded in majestically as Joy to the World and other carols lifted my soul.

However, at home things were growing darker. We were not deterred by this — at first.

Christmas day arrived with the usual flurry of stockings and presents; the dark, long afternoons brought sleep to most of us. The turkey and all that went with it percolated in the oven and on top of the stove. When my godparents arrived, more gifts in hand, the feast was served. All of us ate until we could no longer move. Mom and my godmother did the dishes, laughing loudly from the kitchen while the rest of us lingered in the living room — a room that was not normally open to us children. Lying under the Christmas tree, in the space where presents once lay, I would burp memories of the weeks and days of Christmas that seemed to dance with the sugar plum fairies in my head.

My mood in the days after Christmas, once I had reached ten, went black along with my mom's. Lethargy and an unwillingness to mingle with my sisters took over me. Christmas had been wonderful; the weeks to come were usually not.

As I now look back at these times, I realize I could enjoy the "up" moments. And I also see in my life as an adult that the ebb and flow of the end of the summer and the rush to Christmas preparations attack me still. I am ever so happy throughout November, making Christmas presents and cards for family and friends, listening to hours and hours of Christmas music on my worn out CD player. But come the beginning of December, I seem to withdraw from every Christmas activity and just sit in my apartment and wait — the long, long uncomfortable wait — for Christmas day to pass. I often am so overcome with depression and anxiety that my misery chokes me. The blackness of the season squeezes every joyous breath from my soul.

Over the past few years, through the wisdom of a nurse in a place I once lived, I was given a tool to make this waiting month more bearable. Never had it occurred to me to invite someone over during this time, as I always expected others to invite me to their homes. Rarely did that invitation happen, as everyone was wrapped up in their own Christmas trials and celebrations.

Once I began inviting friends and family to come celebrate a moment or two with me, my depression lightened. Although I still suffer from the Christmas blues, even at age 67, there is much more hope and joy seeping in. Christmas for me is celebrated in November — and I do really kick my heels up during that time.

But that was all knowledge gained with time.

4 SCHOOL

Then school happened. Awkward and miserable, I was sent off to Grade 1 on a September morning, dressed in new clothes brought back from nearby Port Angeles.

That August — and for many years after — had been spent travelling. We drove onto the Coho ferry in Victoria's downtown, and 90 minutes later we were in the U.S. First we would head down to California, via the Oregon coast, returning through the Peace Arch crossing south of Vancouver. Then we would drive to the Okanagan before returning home, camping most of the way.

Clothes were cheaper in Port Angeles and my mother was determined to save money by getting our back-to-school clothes there. But there was a strict limit on the value of goods you could bring back to Canada. My mom's solution was to dress my sisters and I in as many new clothes as possible, putting on layers of shirts and sweaters and dresses in the August heat. She wouldn't declare the purchases when we returned to Canada, and the customs guards never seemed to notice the three bloated children propped up in the back seat of the car. Somehow, we always made it through customs unscathed.

I hated camping. Dragging out a heavy, huge canvas tent that took more than an hour to put up, and then having to sleep in this smelly tent was not my idea of a holiday. When it rained, as it often did, I would roll up against the tent unconsciously while asleep, and water would leach through the canvas and soak me and my sleeping bag. I also hated bugs, campfire smoke and pit toilets. All of these things made my skin crawl and my body stink. I was not amused by smelling bad and scratching mosquito bites all the time.

But my biggest dislike was the constant bickering between my parents as we drove each day. There was nowhere to hide, and out of a sheer need to keep my soul together I learned to daydream and block out the discord. I was always glad to sit in the backseat by the window behind my mom's seat — dad always seemed to drive — because I could just peer out at the passing landscape. They would fight about directions, where to eat, where to camp, would we get there before dark. They fought about almost everything. My sisters and I, imitating our parents, constantly fought in the back seat as well. Joan was the boss and she seemed to rule the roost. One time I remember Anne and I got back at her when she had fallen asleep in the car. Joan always slept with her mouth open, so this one time we stuffed it full of Kleenex. She woke up with a start and very angry. Anne and I, of course, just laughed. We had a one up on our older sister, and I know I felt chuffed.

I was always glad when we got to stay in a house with a real bed and a bathtub, often with our Great Aunt Peggy and Uncle Charlie in Los Angeles or our Aunt Flo, Uncle John and first cousins in San Diego. I often found places I could distance myself from my parents, and one of these places was in our pitched tent in their backyard. I would curl up and read the time away, feeling happy to have my soul back to myself.

More and more, not just in the car, I withdrew into my own fantasy world, imagining a different life — and with increasing frequency invented scenarios where my parents just suddenly died. I never thought my daydreams were unnatural. I assumed all children dreamed these spooky things. Mostly I just wanted dad and mom to fall off a cliff or get run over by a car. I thought I could go away to a fairyland and be looked after by my Fairy Godmother once they were gone for good. Naturally, nothing untoward happened to either parent, and I was stuck with them my entire young life.

Coming back from holidays was like returning from war. And after this month-long summer ordeal, school started.

From my first day in Grade 1, I hated school. As much as I disliked my home life, I hated school even more.

Four women taught in the Quadra Primary School about three blocks from our house, one for each of the four classrooms. Prim and proper they were, with starched pinafores and voices. They seemed ancient to me, like something out of the 1899 Girl's Own Annual that my first grade teacher, Miss Lemmox, gave me on my eighth birthday. Miss Lemmox, a dear old soul who always had a clean hanky dangling from her sleeve cuff, taught Grade 1. She was so kind and thoughtful to my classmates and me. Every day, at recess, just after having our bottle of milk, she would watch us play, chuckling out loud now and again as we discovered new games like tetherball, hopscotch, tag and Red Rover. We were so awkward with our short legs and bodies. I had played some of these games at home, especially tag, but sharing the activity with new friends made me feel shy and embarrassed. I found making my body move in the presence of other people difficult, and so I always seemed to drag my feet or stand rigidly at the edge of the playground. Miss Lemmox always had something wonderfully encouraging to say to me as I re-entered the school after our break. She seemed like a fairy godmother to me and I adored her.

I was, looking back at photos of me at this age, quite smiley and eager looking. Though I always felt under a huge cloud of shame and doubt, I had learned early to hide any emotions that were not pleasant, such as sorrow and anger. My eyes always seemed to sparkle in the photos and I presented a picture of health with soft-looking skin; large brown eyes with long, dark lashes; short, chestnut, always-curled hair (my mom put Anne and I through roller torment every evening); rosy cheeks; and a big, innocent looking smile.

When I look at these photos, I wonder how I could have been living a life of daydreams and broken trusts. I did not look like I was suffering at all. I always wore dresses, no long pants in either winter or summer in those days, and I always felt like a girl then, with a satisfied feeling which did not carry on into my adult years. I do not remember Joan being on the school grounds with me, though I am sure she was in Grade 4. Our four-room schoolhouse, with a large, echoing basement, creaked and moaned at every movement, including the wind. I would dream that the school was haunted with ghosts set to pop out of the walls whenever I passed. Though I believe now that the ghostly figures were based on people who were like my sister Joan, dominating and harsh.

My first day in Grade 1, I walked with my mom, frightened, the three blocks to the school. I shuffled off in my neatly ironed dress and polished shoes to join the other children. I remember the loud, clanging of the school hand bell, and how startled I was. I felt like I was a cow being called into be milked when it didn't want to be. Not only did the bell force us to finish our playtime, we were also made to stand in lines — one for the boys, one for the girls — and wait to enter the school. We were not allowed to intermingle, which puzzled me even then. One by one the boys marched into one door of the school and one by one the girls marched into another. I guess I learned right then and there that "never the twain shall meet." Somehow the boys and the girls were allowed in the same classroom with each other, but not to enter the school or take off our coats and boots together.

Even though I hated school, I was a people pleaser. I'd learned to do anything to make people like me, and I worked hard, harder and hardest to be good at it.

And after all, school was another excuse to leave home.

I excelled in school, particularly reading and drawing. We spent all day in one classroom and all our learning came from one teacher. Grade 1 was Miss Lemmox; Grade 2 Mrs. Smith; Grade 3, Mrs. Goodwin and, lastly, Grade 4 Miss Bossie. I struggled to learn to print, using up any eraser on the end of my pencil in short order. We often did gluing projects, like making Valentine and Christmas chains from construction paper, and I quickly discovered that white paste tasted yummy. My mom, angrily wondering how I went through so much paste in the year, grumpily exclaimed "What did you do, eat it?"

Nothing untoward ever happened to me during my first four years at Quadra Primary, except the chewing gum incident. I enjoyed chewing gum. One day, in Grade 2, my exasperated teacher, tired of hearing me pop my wad of gum, grabbed me and dragged me to the front of the classroom, making a spectacle and example of me for breaking the rule of "no gum in the confines of the school grounds and building." Humiliated, I was forced to spend the rest of the afternoon standing in front of the class with the gum stuck to my nose. The punishment didn't stop me from chewing gum after that, but I never blew bubbles again.

When the last day of June happened that very first year, I was ever so glad to be free of the rigid schedules. There was a joy in having the chance to be alone once again. This freedom did not last for many years. My mom, when I was about eight years old, and every year after, arranged that Joan and I, (and later Anne) would spend July picking berries at a farm in the country to earn money for our holidays. We had to get up at the hint of dawn to be on the farm bus by 6:30 a.m.. This was backbreaking work, and even though we were close to the ground as children, all the bending hurt after a while, and the hot sun burned away my energy very quickly. I was a slow picker and never made much money, at least until Anne started picking. Then she would often stop her plucking berries to help me out. I was always tired, heaping myself into bed when the bus dropped us at home. I learned quickly that physical labour and I never got along.

5 LIFE CHANGES

I'm 10. It's Dec. 27, 1960, Tuesday, two days after Christmas.

It's an unusually warm and sunny day. I'm walking home from the dentist downtown, thinking about nothing but satisfaction. No cavities. A polished smile. What better news could I have, having eaten so many sweets and goodies over Christmas?

Quadra-Hillside, our neighbourhood, still seemed on the city's edge in those days. I decided to cut through a vacant lot, all rocky outcrops, on my way home. Today, it's swallowed up by the city, the site of the Save-On-Foods Memorial Centre, Victoria's arena, which replaced the old Memorial Arena.

For years the neighbourhood kids played hide and seek on the rocks behind the arena, while the older teens snuck a few impromptu "smoochies" behind the bigger outcrops. I liked to play there, climbing and hiding in the impressive rock formations.

Until one day my enthusiasm for this natural playground came to an abrupt and painful halt, and my life — innocent and carefree in many ways, despite our troubled family — was shattered forever. There was, to be sure, agony in my first decade, but I still felt hope, I was alive to the possibility of change and redemption. That ended.

As I climbed the hill from the arena parking lot, chuffed with myself, there was a man standing at the top. His long raincoat, which brushed the ground, was held wide open and a huge grin slashed his face. He had no clothes on under the coat. His obvious pleasure sickened yet fascinated me.

Not knowing what to do, I walked toward him with the idea of passing. However, as I approached he let go of the coat and grabbed both my hands tightly with one hand while covering my mouth with his other. Yanking me up the rocks, as I struggled without success to escape, a child against a grown man, he found a well of grass hidden between two outcroppings and pushed me down onto it. He whispered, telling me to keep my head down and my mouth shut. From underneath his raincoat he pulled out his penis and started to, as I learned later in life, masturbate. The horrible look of pleasure on his face made me cringe in fear. After what seemed like only a few seconds the man crawled toward me, I guess needing his head to not rise over the rocks, grabbed me, pulled my underwear down with a forceful tug and stuck his fingers up my vagina and then, painfully, excruciatingly painfully, he stuck his penis inside of me and thrust himself until this disgusting white, milky stuff came pouring out of my private parts. Horror overtook me.

Somehow I gained the energy to pull up my panties and run, painfully hurtling over the rocks as though they did not exist. My mouth was dry. I was in full panic as I ran, turning to look behind me in terror to make sure he wasn't following me.

The house was empty when I arrived home. I fled into the bathroom; taking a face cloth I scrubbed and scrubbed my genital area with soap and water. Knowing that I could never tell my mom what happened, I changed my clothes, combed my hair and spent a few minutes trying to erase the panic from my body and face.

I had lived with secrets — my consumption of pills, the self-strangulation and genital mutilation. This new secret, the one I could never tell anyone, welled up in my ten-year-old soul. The physical and emotional pain was more than I could tolerate, and I crawled even further into the safety of my dreaming mind. I crawled into a black hole that has never seemed to have gone away.

Sleep had never been a problem for me, despite the worries and fears of my waking hours. I could fall asleep anywhere and wake up refreshed. But that night, horrendous nightmares tormented me, ones that continued most nights after. Insomnia began to haunt me. To this day I still have nightmares, and insomnia and I are very good friends.

However, this is not the end of this story.

About a week later, I was riding my bike home from Brownies in the dark of an early January evening. I saw the same man and, terrified, I pushed harder and faster on the pedals of my two-wheeler. My terror overwhelmed me as he started chasing me on foot, whistling this horrible whistle and yelling out "Stop, stop." I pedalled harder and harder, trying not to look back. I reached home and, driven by the fear that my mom would find out about this man, I opened the garage door, pushed my bicycle in quickly and shut the door behind me. I still heard his whistle as I cringed against the spider-webbed garage wall, shaking uncontrollably, as I waited for what seemed like hours and hours. When the whistling had stopped for a long, long time, I lifted the garage door and fled into the house. My mom, so angry at me for being very late, took the long leather belt she kept in the corner drawer of the kitchen cabinets and whacked me over my bum. My screams rang through the night until, crying frantically, I ran to my room.

From then on, whenever I was in the house, I would lie down on the living room floor, face down, lost in a world of fantasy, protected by nothing but solitude, and, a short time later, music. I could not speak much anymore. I felt dirty and my shame would not go away. My nightmares continued, sleepwalking began, and my terror that my mom would find out what I had done consumed me.

A year later, I said to my mom, quietly, and in great fear: "A man touched me." My mom screamed at me, grabbed me by the hand as she phoned the local police station. Somehow, in her own rage, she knew what had happened to me. The police were at our front door within minutes. They tried to get my story out of me; in bits and stumbling pieces, I tried to tell them what had happened and to describe the man. Mostly I couldn't do either of these things. The police left and my mom immediately phoned our family physician to check out my body.

Once this had been done, she took me aside, still angry, and ordered me to "never tell another soul and to never speak of this again." I was thrown into a world of silence, living with the secret I could never tell anyone. For years and years, I held this secret — all the while enduring more and more abuse at home from the other deranged people in my life.

6 BEGINNING OF FAITH

"We do not presume to come to this thy Table, O merciful Lord. Trusting in our own righteousness, But in thy manifold and great mercies. We are not worthy So much as to gather up the crumbs under thy Table. But thou art the same Lord, Whose property is always to have mercy: Grant us therefore, gracious Lord, so to eat the Flesh of thy dear Son Jesus Christ, and to drink his blood, That our sinful bodies may be made clean by his Body, And our souls washed through his most precious Blood, And that we may evermore dwell in him, And he in us. Amen."

The Book of Common Prayer (Anglican) 1962

When I was a young child my father would transport both Joan and me to church every Sunday morning in the huge metal basket of his bicycle. The basket's frame dug into our derrieres and our crotches as we bumped along the 10-block ride, yet I was so happy for the outing with my dad — even though he slept noisily through the actual church service.

Both Joan and I had been baptized as babes in arms at St. John the Divine Anglican Church in Victoria. Our godparents, Dot and Maurie, were there for the christenings, promising to keep a spiritual eye on the two of us throughout our lifetimes and to see that no harm came to us.

Something about this, at least with our godfather, went wrong not long after these sacred vows were made.

I found solace in attending church. When I reached age six or seven

I joined the choristers at St. John's. I loved the company and silliness during our weekly practices and the rituals of the Sunday service. But most of all, I looked forward to the freedom to be away from home twice a week, to flee the angry rooms at home and be among other kids with similar interests. Joining the choir set me on a road to a new way to profess my faith — through this music. The drama of the hymns and the anthems filled my soul with a new kind of hope and I wasn't afraid to sing out my passion and my pain. I literally grew up in the choir — though I am sure maturity was not one of my strong points. I joined the adult choir in my teens and started on a more demanding spiritual and musical journey. This time sparked my intense interest in choral spiritual music, which I still enjoy.

The church became real to me, so real that I found myself talking to God and Jesus at all hours of the day and night. I had found solace in the rituals, the music we sang, the prayers.

Each Sunday morning, garbed in my red cassock with a white ruffle collar, I proudly but penitently paraded down the centre aisle of the sanctuary, where services were always held, toward the choir stalls at the east end of the church. The choir stalls were just shy of the chancel where the altar was barricaded behind a railing and my favourite stained glass window proudly portrayed Jesus holding a lamb, shepherd's crook in one hand and the sheep tenderly nestled in his other arm. In joyousness I lifted my voice up, in both prayer and song, to fill the high ceiling. I knew God was there, somewhere, and He could hear me clearly, above everyone else. I was particularly taken by the words above, part of the Communion service in which wine and bread substituted for the blood and body of Christ.

Despite the words about mercy, I felt God could be a fiercely punitive man and I would cower at the altar when I said my prayers. I was afraid of the wrath of God because I was too timid to try and "gather up the crumbs under His table." Even after getting confirmed at 13 and entering my teens, I never lost my respect for the liturgy.

But I was scared to death of Canon George Biddle, the church minister, and his almost archaic ways — he spoke with passion but with a hint of egotism. He often stood, stoically, with his arms propped in the air, exuding authority and penitence. His robes, cassock all white with a stole that indicated the church season (red for Advent, green for Trinity, white for Christmas and Easter), hung perfectly from his broad shoulders. Kneeling before the altar week after week made me more penitential and on the day of Confirmation I managed to survive the ordeal of kneeling before Bishop Harold Sexton and Canon Biddle at the front altar. The Bishop, with his heavy, awe-inspiring hand, huge papal-type ring attached to his left middle finger, welcomed me into God's fold as an adult ready to carry on the vows of my Baptism.

When I was about 11 or 12, I began to go to church every Sunday evening on my own, walking in the dark, unafraid. (This fearlessness would soon be stolen from me.)

Evensong made me swoon and I would fight my parents to be allowed to go every week. After all, God expected me to go and I did not want to add another sin to my huge list by not attending and worshipping him. Again I was swayed by prayer, this time the prayer of Confession that began "Almighty and most merciful Father, We have erred and strayed from thy ways like lost sheep, We have followed the devices and desires of our own heart, We have offended against thy holy laws..." I did not want to be a lost sheep.

What I realized I needed so desperately from God was forgiveness and love. I felt I was responsible for the mess at home and that if I could be a better person, family life would become normal. The more I prayed, the more hurt I became because He just did not seem to be answering my prayers and I was unable to reach His high expectations of me — no matter how hard I tried.

Yet I held on to the belief that, if I prayed harder and harder and longer and longer each day, God would hear me and make "all things new," as promised in the prayer book. Each day, month, year, my desperation increased. The pain in my heart was at times totally unbearable. My sins, I realized, were overtaking me... even though I did not really know what sins were.

When I was about 12, on Remembrance Day, which was on a Sunday, I sat in Morning Prayer and, as the Last Post was being sounded, I remember asking myself: What does it really feel like to die? I was weary from life at home and I wanted peace in my heart. When I went home that afternoon I rooted around in the medicine chest and found a full bottle of aspirin. Waiting until darkness had sunk over the earth, I took the whole bottle of pills, knowing that I would be going to Evensong in a few minutes, hoping I would die in church. I put on my winter coat over my still neatly pressed dress, shoved my hands into my gloves, then staggered my way to church, feeling very sick to my stomach and my ears ringing loudly—so loud I could not even hear the city sounds. Occasionally I would stop by the curb and vomit a little because my stomach really hurt. I wanted to be taken by God, right away, that evening. Dying in church would be the ultimate sacrifice I could offer for my sins.

The church, almost empty, was chilly and very, very dark. The hanging orange lights did not seem to fill the vaulted void of the ceiling. The images on the stained glass could not be seen, except for the Good Shepard over the chancel. There was a light behind the window to show it off. Shortly after I entered the Sanctuary, I passed out. I was scooped up and taken into the washroom in the hallway near the church office. By the time I was revived, one of the parishioners, a nurse, realized that I had somehow attempted suicide and had me leaning over the bathroom toilet retching out my guts. She rushed me to the hospital in her car. In Emergency I was dosed with medicine and charcoal and minutes later was chucking out black, putrid vomit, leaving a burning sensation in both my stomach and my throat.

Evensong always started at 7 p.m., and I must have been in the emergency ward by around 7:30. Moving from unconsciousness to consciousness, I lay on a cot in the ward. After I had finish emptying my stomach, the hospital phoned my mom to come and pick me up. Neither the hospital staff nor my mom, when she came and collected me from the emergency ward, had any compassion for me. They all made it clear I had committed a huge crime.

My mom, totally disgusted with my plight, yanked me by the arm, tightly and angrily, and then pushed me out the Emergency Room doors.

Mom's response to my suicide attempt? Disgust and humiliation. She kept repeating to me "How could you do this to ME?" What would her friends say? As she cruelly continued to grab me by the arm and shoved me out the Emergency Room doors, with a husky, out-of-breath, threatening voice she told me that she really should be calling the police to put me in jail "because that is where I belonged." In the '60s, suicide attempts were a criminal offence and jail was the penalty. Inside of myself, I secretly wished that my mother would have more compassion and caring for me than that — maybe I did need to go to jail.

How humiliated I felt. Crushed, believing that I had angered her and God, I concluded that I had one choice — that I must try again until I successfully passed on to Heaven and the hereafter I knew was waiting.

Suicide attempts became a lifelong act of penitence and hope. Dying for the sake of forgiveness was my only chance of being redeemed in the eyes of God and my mother.

That night sleep was disturbed and distorted. White hollow rings floated through my head and I fell from one ring to another. I felt so nauseous, but I did not want to ask my mom for help. All night, floating back and forth between rings and dreams, I began to hate myself more. I needed the wrath of God to force me to change my ways; yet, more and more, I pleaded with God to take me — and to make it soon

7 SECRETS

My rape by the trench-coated stranger was traumatic, but other sexual abuse, closer to home, was part of my life. Maurie, the godfather who had promised to protect us when we were baptized, molested and raped me over many, many years.

I remember the times he had me sit on his lap, my dress prettily covering his abdomen and upper legs. Without fail he would stick his fingers up into my vagina, right there in front of my parents, my siblings and his wife.

I had always been afraid of getting in trouble if I made a scene, so as much as I hated the intrusion of my body, for many years I did not say anything or run. My parents thought it was "cute" to see me sitting on Maurie's lap. Eventually, going to my godparents' home or having them come to mine made me feel sick to my stomach and fearful. Finally, one day, I jumped off his lap and screamed at him to leave me alone. My parents did not bat an eye and carried on their conversation. The assaults didn't stop.

Maurie, and my dad when with him, took great pleasure in tickling the feet of my sisters and I. It was not a game for me; they were sadists. Unable to escape their grasp, I laughed uncontrollably and writhed in pain, screaming "STOP, stop." They just held on tighter and tighter and increased the torture, as if they wanted to inflict more and more suffering. All the while Maurie, in particular, could look down my dress into my crotch, with deep pleasure scored onto his leering face. What surprised me most was that neither my mom nor my godmother would stop this behaviour by both my godfather and my dad. Instead, they would laugh and laugh with them. I began to hate my mother more and more.

My mom met Dot in the Women's Army Corp during the war. They were stationed, I believe, near Winnipeg together. After the war, when my mom and dad moved to Victoria, Dot, now married to Maurie, reunited with her good friend. Because Dot was gentle, endearing and just a plain decent person, my mom must have trusted her. Dot held a position at Henry Birks and Sons, a jewelry store at the corner of Douglas and Yates in Victoria. I cannot remember what Maurie did, except I knew he was a "white collar worker." A true business man, up and coming in his world of desk work and prestige.

My godparents would often have me over to their house for a pajama party after an adventure with them during the day. When I was in their home overnight, I shivered in my bed in the spare bedroom. Without fail, Maurie would crawl into bed with me to "help me" go to sleep. My godmother either did not know or chose not to act — she never intervened. Perhaps she felt helpless and unable to stop her husband from inflicting himself upon me. When they both eventually died — Dot by leukemia and Maurie by old age — I could not look back on these sexual "adventures" without pain and anger. When Maurie died, I refused to go to his funeral because I hated him so, so much.

Then there was my dad. I hated him as well, more and more as the years went by. When I was around him, either with other people or by myself, there was an evil shimmer in his eyes. He would pucker his mouth and yank me to his body, with this great urgency for me to kiss him on the lips. Not only was the kiss sickening to me, but his grip on my arm was crushing and painful. He appeared to take great delight in forcing pain upon me, my sisters, my mom and anyone else in the room. He seemed to think this was funny, as we all writhed in pain and tried to escape. He just would not let go until tears and screams filled the room. Until then he just laughed and laughed and laughed.

There were other instances of molestation in my life. and other types of unwanted sexual encounters. However, I wish to protect those who intruded on my body. Most of these acts, I believe, were done in a reaction to confusion, tortured thoughts and innocence. I do not wish to harm the persons involved.

But to this day I refuse to kiss anyone, particularly on the lips. And I wince at the thought of any sexual encounter with a man. Even thoughts of making babies repulses me, and I am angry all the time when I see pregnant women, secretly chastising them for the means they had to use to achieve their budding state. I cannot be around babies without feeling hostile and dirty. When I was in my late thirties, I was banned from holding my oldest nephew when he was a baby because I would shake him in anger. That anger came from my own experiences, from the stranger, Maurie and others. I was relieved when I no longer had to hold my nephew after that. About five years later, I would pay a high price for my confusion and uncertainty about my relationship with my young nephew. Secrets heaped upon secrets.

These experiences changed the course of my life. I never married, had a sexual relationship with a man, had babies. I wiggled my way out of kissing men. Having had a couple of "boyfriends" in my teen years, I lost them because I would not, among other things, kiss them. I really did not want a boyfriend, but my mom felt it was necessary. I had come to believe that kissing made babies, which added to my horror when my dad grabbed me and demanded a kiss. My mom, throughout our teen years, regularly threatened to kill any one of my sisters and me if we got pregnant. And I came to believe that kissing could bring death. Funnily enough, I did not want to die from someone else's hand — it did not seem part of my ultimate sacrifice.

By the time I was in my late teens, I was in and out of hospital. My trips to the hospital were never helpful because, for years and years, I was unable to talk to the nurses or the other patients. I was mute, living in a world of fear and silence. My acts of abuse toward myself became more and more intense. Not only was I cutting my genitals but I was also overdosing more and more. Head banging became a way for me to deal with the pains of abuse.

Throughout this time, I often looked to church for comfort, but my attendance was erratic because I had really no one church I was attending during that time. I was a religious drifter and the church didn't play a large role in my mental and spiritual healing at that time.

I trusted no one — hospital staff, ministers, parents or myself. I was so totally alone in my thoughts then, running away from them by curling up on my bed and refusing to move or searching for other methods to cover up the pain. I had no insight into my mental illness and was ruled totally by it. And, from this place of pain, an addiction began to grow.

But once I wrote these pages for this book on how sexual abuse had affected me, this act of writing broke the silence and those horrible, soul-eating secrets and pain mysteriously fled my body and I began to feel light and absolved.

Perhaps now I can move on with my life — at age 67. I doubt that I would enter into any kind of relationship now, but sometimes I wonder what my life would have been like if I had married, had children and, eventually, rested peacefully next to a spouse on a cold winter night.

I doubt that I will ever know.

8 UNRAVELLING

My fifth and six grades are a blur. I had withdrawn further and further into my own world. Somehow on the surface I appeared to be functioning as a shy 10-year-old. Underneath I was wracked with fears and pain.

My life really started to unravel around the time I entered Grade 7 at S.J. Willis Junior High, a 15-minute walk from our house. I always felt that I came from "the wrong side of the tracks" and was embarrassed to be one of the poor folk who attended the school.

Not until later in my adult life did I appreciate that my parents tried hard to keep poverty from barking at our door, in large part by holding many jobs that they seemed unsuited for to put food on our table and clothes on our back.

My mom, not having Grade 12, worked at hot dog stands at Thetis Lake and the Royal Athletic Park in summer months and picked up odd jobs during the winter, finally ending up at Roger's Chocolates shop on Government Street as a dipper. She took pride in this position because her "signature" on each chocolate she dipped went to destinations all around the world.

Eventually she moved into a position that had benefits as a dietary aid at the Royal Jubilee Hospital. Her many previous jobs prepared her for the extremely hard work of preparing meals and doing dishes for the patients in the hospital. I thought she was better suited for this job, because the employer did not take advantage of her hard work and loyalties. My dad's part-time plumbing positions kept him busy at something he did not want to do. He had higher aspirations but contented himself plugging along doing this work.

Not only did my parents supply the basics for decent living, my mom also provided funds to help us develop hobbies and attend programs such as Brownies, Guides and Sea Rangers — and the school orchestra for me. While I didn't understand then the gigantic efforts my parents put forth to keep up the middle class image, I have to admit now that they did a fantastic job. It's too bad that as a child I could not see how they worked to not just make do, but provide for our family. Mom and dad sacrificed a lot for me — and now I am glad, because I feel like a person in the middle class because of their efforts, even though I live below the poverty line. There is somewhat of a "polish" about me that was nurtured by them.

My dreams, always vivid, now took a different direction, often exploring death in new forms, especially being floated down a river on a burning pyre, an idea taken from a poem or story we studied in school. Images from my developing spiritual life started to appear in more dreams. I dreamed I was a hart, peacefully feeding on a river bank, or I was laying down in green pastures, the cool, gentle breeze brushing against me. Many of my joyful dreams came from church, sparked by the ethereal pomp and circumstance of "My soul does magnify the Lord" from the Book of Common Prayer, along with chants and joyful pieces from hymns such as "The Lord is King! Lift up thy voice" or "O for a thousand tongues to sing." There was drama, and there was despair, intertwined with hope.

In my waking hours, I was trapped in a mind and a life that hurt. I found solace in Grade 7 by falling in love with my English teacher.

When I entered junior high, a longing that has stayed with me most of my life emerged. I desperately wanted someone to care about me, to save me from myself and my family, to listen to me and free me from the inner horrors that I could not speak of to anyone.

I couldn't share this need with anyone. So I was hurtled into a quest, one that I have only recognized in these past few years of my life. My desperate desire for rescue caused me, throughout my life, to do sometimes outrageous and desperate things.

My feelings for my teacher, so private and so shameful, led me to write to him for three years, almost daily.

The typewriter in the basement became my ally. I hammered out my feelings, my woes, my soul to him. I needed him to love me back; I needed him to help me. My typing grew faster and faster so my letter-writing would not be found out. I did not want my mom or sisters to know that I had this love for him. Clandestinely, I wrote to him day after day: poetry and page after page of longing flowed from my fingertips. Each evening, before sundown, I would slink off to the mailbox and drop unspoken pleas for help into the large red box.

I longed for freedom from the world around me, and somehow I believed this love would accomplish that goal. I didn't know how this could happen, but I just kept on believing.

All the typing I did secretly day after day helped me win "The Fastest First Year Typist" award in Grade 10. My need to type quickly and accurately at home meant that when it came to test typing skills in class I could throw the carriage back and forth on the manual typewriter to the clatter of 93 words per minute, with less than two errors. Sometimes good things do come out of the bad — and I had the trophy to prove it.

Then my dreams of rescue, of escape, came to an end. My adored teacher, after three years of my letters, phoned me at home to tell me he was moving to France. My mother answered, but she never asked me who had called, or why, and I never offered her the information. I think she knew about my fixation on this teacher, because later on in Grade 7 she introduced me to some pen pals, I expect to distract me from him.

As I hung up the telephone, my world shattered. I had no one to turn to anymore. The blackness deepened within me and I withdrew even more from the world around me.

That was the only time the teacher spoke to me in a way that acknowledged my letters. I'm still angry — perhaps even more angry in recent years — that he never even talked to me or offered to help. I am sure he never read most of the letters, but if he had read even one, and taken action, perhaps I would have taken a different path, one that would have taken me away from the bleak dark road I was on to a place with freedom and mental health. Perhaps I would have had an opportunity to gain an understanding of my life, and learned that I could change my destiny by developing mental wisdom and confidence.

Instead, I was again on the lookout for someone else to love, someone to listen to me, and, most importantly, someone to love me back. This venture with my English teacher hurtled me into travelling even darker turns in my road. These injuries of my soul became unbearable; my loneliness overwhelmed me.

Feeling so helpless and so unhinged by my teacher's departure, which I thought was to spite me and to run away from my intrusion into his life, I chose to reach out to another teacher almost immediately.

"I will not let you fall in love with me," he responded. "Go away."

Hurt and despairing once again, I felt that I had been set adrift on that burning pyre, floating down the river with my soul on fire — anger and hate forcing into hiding every aspect of my life from those around me. Images of my rape flooded my brain, and nights were filled with the shame and disgust that had grown within me while I had been writing my teacher. Feelings of abandonment consumed me, and my suicide attempt in church at 14 foreshadowed the life that I would lead.

My guilt and shame drove my spiritual life, which became my hope for repentance and forgiveness, neither which happened. My faith in God and Jesus, my need for them, became the most important thing in my life. I watched the popular TV show "The Flying Nun" and the movie "A Nun's Story" and saw refuge in a convent of other women who would nurture me with their love and caring. I decided I could be a nun and a nurse at the same time and find hope. Yes, that is what I wanted to do.

Through my teenage years, books and music took hold of me and held me firmly in their grasp. My reading was driven by my desire to become a nurse. I devoured all books that helped me envision that dream — the Cherry Ames series of novels about a mystery-solving young nurse, stories about Florence Nightingale and Madame Curie and many, many other true life medical stories. The books brought a sacredness to my nursing dream, and offered hope that calmed me. Still, all my reading and dreaming never led to a medical career. At one point in my teenage life I was a candy striper at St. Joseph's hospital looking after aged nuns. This experience made me want even more to be a nurse. But this dream never came to fruition.

After the loss of my teacher, I spent hours laying on the floor in our living room (I do not know why I had dispensation to be in that room, usually reserved for company), listening to classical record albums over and over again. Because I loved classical music, my parents had given me violin lessons. I appreciated the musical world in a way that no one else seemed to share — not my family, or schoolmates —

but never could master the violin. However, we did have those records from Safeway. The music would transport me to a heaven that seemed full of light, love and peace.

More and more, as I listened to this music, I was rent apart by a paradox: I wanted to be a nurse, yet I also wanted to enter "the Kingdom of Heaven." And I wanted to do both immediately!

Death wishes consumed me more and more. I was abusing myself, often by taking huge handfuls of pills to numb my painful feelings. These pills made me delightfully sick to my stomach — a type of penitence. I began the ritual of banging my head on the walls, at first a few times in a row occasionally, then, as the years went by, more often and with many more blows. I even slashed my wrist at one point and, while having it sewn shut at the hospital, I was chastised by the nurse for seeking attention, even though I did everything in secret. She ordered me sent home. My dad didn't take much heed of my situation but my mom collected me from the hospital with another loud reprimand and another threat of sending me to the police. By this time, I was used to my mom's threats and I just went quietly along with her, my wrist throbbing from the stitches.

Odd habits consumed me. I started drinking things like bleach and iodine, eating nails and whatever else I could get my hands on. The pains in my stomach were necessary to reach God's mercy. I needed my sins to be washed away by Him.

I had been sent to a psychiatrist when I was 14. My mom was angry when she was called to the hospital after my first major suicide attempt, but heeded — at least initially — the emergency room physician's advice to seek psychiatric help for me to sort out my thoughts and feelings.

She took me to the first appointment with Dr. Ian Kenning, a tall skinny man with a huge smile on his face, and then later to Dr. Hackett, a kindly, slightly rotund, elderly gentleman also with a huge smile, both of whose practices were at the Medical Arts Building on Pandora. Both times the sessions were unproductive because I would not talk, especially after my mom proclaimed loudly in the waiting room the first time I saw Dr. Kenning that all I really needed was a strap across my backside. I believe I went for a few sessions before my mom pulled me out. Later on, within the year, I was to see Dr. Hackett, but again he was pulled from my repertoire of potential help soon after I began my sessions with him. There was to be no more counselling until I reached 18. I suspect that my mom did not want the "dirty laundry" of my home life to be aired, seeking to protect her dignity and her secrets.

Throughout all these twists and turns in my life, I never had much hope. My church associations, the choir particularly, became my passion, and the rituals of the services became my life guides. The organ music massaged my soul Sunday after Sunday.

And, eventually, the minister at St. John's replaced my teachers as my hope for help and love.

This led to the biggest fork in my road, one that it altered my hopes and dreams for the next 45 years of my life.

9 FLAMES

My quest for love and for help led me to seek out the new minister at St. John the Divine.

My life was not improving. In fact, my 16th year was wrought with more pain and more secrets. My mom was herding me back and forth to the doctor because she believed I had not yet started my period and she wanted to know why. The reality was I had begun menstruating, but was ashamed of the fact and had told no one. There was something unspeakably dirty about this process, and I did not understand it at all. The loss of blood scared me, as, I later learned, it scared so many young women. I hid my bloody underwear wherever I could find a safe place to conceal them. Even sex education, such as it was, with a black-and-white movie projected on the school wall, did nothing to ease my angst around this. I did not understand any of this "growing up" process, and I wished it would go away and leave me alone. And, furthermore, to admit to my mom this horrible "grown up" disorder was happening to me — no way!

I thought God would sort out all this need for love and compassion, and I wanted to leave it up to the St. John's minister, Grahame Baker. He wasn't old — perhaps 40 — and seemed cheerful and green enough to be a good listener and rescue me from my depths.

I was more and more alone. Interactions with my family, teachers and others were too painful and my secrets, the rapes, the abuses, were too scarring to speak of. I isolated myself, sinking into more and more blackness.

Although I had never envisioned a "man of God" as a potential lover or a means of transporting myself out of my blackness into the Light of Christ, something inside of me, desperate and lonely, reached out.

I turned again to the typewriter in the basement. More secret letters addressed to the minister started to fill up the mailbox on the corner of my street. I wrote about the misery of my life — but not with any specifics about my family life. I was living in this fantasy world and was unable to reach out in any concrete way, such as saying "Will you help me find happiness?" or "Can you help me be closer to God?" I am sure most of what I wrote was a youth's plea to have someone listen, even though I was never sure of what to say or write. I wrote about the part I played in the mess of my family situation, still believing that I was the one responsible for the breakdown of my family.

I was too frightened to approach the minister in person. So I did not know that for some two years, as I poured out my heart and soul in letters, he did not have a clue who I was. We never had been introduced and I remained in the holy background at church.

But I still believed the minister offered me a new hope that somehow I would be raised up into the safe realm of God.

Two years of these letters passed and my faith started to lift me up. Somehow my letters to this holy man purged my soul of other lusts and other false hopes. My interest in the Good Friday and Easter stories evolved. I was Christ. I was crucified and I was raised up three days later. The passion experienced left me in ethereal ecstasy. Like Christ, I felt the torture and the redemption. I knew I would be finally saved from my pain: after all, wasn't Christ saved on Easter Sunday? Why would I not be just like him?

But sometime in my 17th year, during a roundtable discussion at one of the meetings in the church hall, I sensed the minister realized that I was "Gayle Chapman," the person who had been sending him all those letters. I knew that he had made the connection between the young woman he had seen in church activities so many times and the letters I had sent.

I was frightened that my identity had been revealed. When an 'aha' expression flashed across his divine face, I felt embarrassed and humiliated, wanting to run and hide. This man knew me now. My letters had a writer, and the person who seemed to stare at him from the choir stalls every Sunday morning now had a name. Oh God, I prayed, let him have compassion.

It was not a surprise that the minister didn't know my name, despite my time in the choir and involvement in church activities. For years I had remained in the background, hiding in the shadows of the church. I carried a dark secret that brought me shame.

About seven years earlier, St. John the Divine Church had been damaged in one of the city's worst fires. And I believed, to my shame, that I had started the fire that gutted this glorious church. It was another secret that weighed upon me.

I was 10 at the time. I recalled being at the church's outside stairwell with a friend, just after finishing up with Brownies for the day. We were gleefully lighting the matches that we carried in a small, silver, cylindrical case on our uniform belt, and throwing the lighted matches onto the pavement. I never took care to notice if the matches burned out or not; however, because I found comfort in this sinful act, I sensed that my sins were being redeemed.

Then I remembered arriving home that evening to find my parents watching a horrendous fire on the television. At first I did not pay much attention. However, within a few minutes I realized it was St. John's, engulfed in flames.

My God, I had set the church on fire. I recalled staring at the television, the horror of my unforgivable act there on the screen. As we watched, I saw the inside of the church being destroyed, the lovely stained glass bursting outwards from the heat, and the wood panels and pews exploding with flames. How could I bear the anxiety and pain I felt as I watched? My sins, I believed, had reached a new level and I withdrew deeper into myself. I felt the wrath of God wrap its cold, angry tentacles around me.

For a year or more, the congregation held services in the church hall, which had not been damaged by the flames. There was more light in the hall and I became self-conscious of being seen as the perpetrator of this disaster. In spite of this, my need for the church and its comfort propelled me to it Sunday after Sunday. As well, my need to keep my secret drove me into a new kind of shyness and a new kind of need.

When the minister glared at me when I said my name that day in the hall, I felt my fate had been sealed. His face told me he knew about me and the fire.

It wasn't until this book was researched that I learned I did not set the fire. It was an electrical fire. It wasn't reported until 4 a.m., so I could not have come home and watched the flames on the television news.

I had been primed all my life, by my parents, to take responsibility for my actions and consequences. I felt guilty whenever anything went wrong, at home or school or anywhere else. Because I was frivolously lighting matches early that evening, I knew right away one of them might not have burned out and then set the basement door on fire. Yes, I was guilty for sure. I truly believed I was the one responsible for this fire and I carried this burden with me for many decades, quietly afraid of being caught and put in jail. I felt this fire put a huge wall between me and the minister, because I dared not to tell him my part in it.

After that day, my letter writing became more intense. I never wrote about the fire, but I wanted to share the pain in my life. I wanted him to help me understand why I felt so unworthy of God's love and so open to God's wrath. I loved this minister more and more. My head swam with scenarios and dreams about him every day. He would save me and make everything right between me and God.

One day I made an appointment to go and see the minister. I was scared and didn't know what I would say or how I would present myself as I shuffled up to the church office.

What could I say? I needed him so, so much. At the appointed time, the minister came to fetch me from the waiting room and we entered into his office, dark, with a choking air about it. Here was my chance to confess my sins and to be atoned. I sat there, the chair uncomfortable and the darkness and stuffiness of the room uniting with the darkness of my soul. I could not speak — not one word. He seemed calm with me sitting there. I remember a half smile on his face, that now I would translate as being patronizing, puzzled and thinking "cute." After about 10 minutes, I left, but made another appointment, and then another the next time we met. Never having the courage to speak, I poured out my wretched soul in letters and more letters.

Finally, the minister, after many months of my fruitless and time-wasting appointments, exclaimed with great anger and disgust (that is how I saw it) that I should leave him alone. No more letters, no more appointments. Leave him alone.

My mind, reeling with this horrendous rejection, sunk even further into its own darkness. I was full of shame, and rage, uncontainable rage. Although I did not know what this feeling was, I told myself that I would get him for pushing me away. He would pay dearly.

I decided, in the minutes after that appointment, that I would have revenge. I would kill him. And that became my undoing. I gave up hope that my tortured soul would ever be redeemed, or my loneliness removed by God. My sins had left me with no place at St. John's.

My life would never be the same.

10 FORSAKEN

My imagined flirtations with teachers and the minister had helped me avoid the reality of my disintegrating home life. As I moved through my teen years, my mom and dad fought more and more. Not only did their arguments grow more frequent, but they were angrier and more and more brutal. They were into physical violence, hitting one another ruthlessly. I would hide in the cupboard when this started to happen each time. Crying, I would try and comfort myself — I do not know what my sisters were doing, but I rocked myself into my own world, staying hidden for hours.

Often I would come home from school or church to find my dad was gone. He either had left, or my mom had thrown him out. Sometimes weeks passed before he would arrive back at our front door, penitent and grovelling, begging for her to take him back. She always did and, for a time life, around the house would resume some normalcy. There was joy and peace inside the walls of our home; hope for a new life prevailed.

This hope never lasted long.

My dad returned home one late fall afternoon excited, and although my mom did not seem happy to see him, she let him into the living room. A few days later, when the tension eased, my dad pulled a small, longish, velvet box from his shirt pocket and slipped it into my mother's hand.

But she didn't want any presents that carried the price tag of forgiveness. She opened the box and lifted out a ruby necklace and matching earrings. She immediately thrust them back into my father's hands with great disdain, yelling that she did not want his gifts.

She seemed insulted, unwilling to repair their relationship this time. I had been crossing my fingers, hoping they would finally end their hostility toward each other. I watched my dad, in obvious despair, hide the velvet box in his top bureau drawer, a high boy, handmade and passed down from his mother. No nails in it; mitred corners and a veneer of oak in very good condition considering it was over forty or fifty years old. (I still have this dresser — for some reason it is very special to me.) The necklace and earrings were never spoken of again. Often I would see my dad secretly opening the box when he thought no one was looking. There was a sadness in his demeanour; perhaps he knew his marriage was on the verge of dissolving or, worse, that one of them would die — perhaps him.

This turmoil — fights and partial reconciliations, the disappearances and reappearances of my dad — made my world more and more unstable. I lived in terror that one time my dad would leave and never come back. When he was gone, I lay awake night after night waiting for him to return. Sleep became more elusive, and when it did come, I was still tormented by nightmares.

I wanted him to come home. Later I knew he was not much of a father to me, but he was my father, and I needed him to guide me through the angry and unpredictable path on which my mom and I travelled.

But he was just like my teacher and my minister, and I realized men could not respond to my need for love and caring. My anger and disdain at the unpredictability of the males in my life hurtled me into behaviours that, even all these years later, I regret. But I hated that I was constantly being abandoned, and as the months went by I began to hate the changes that were happening within our family. I sensed the doom of my family's life.

But my burning anger was focused on my agonizing rejection by the minister. He didn't just abandon me; God had abandoned me. I had prayed and prayed that God would use the minister as a vehicle to save me from the fiery waters of hell. Now I had sunk deeper into this pit. There would be no help. I knew I had to fight to be alive. My anger at what seemed a violent ending to my only hopes threw me into a tailspin.

I developed my plan as I walked hastily home from the meeting with the minister that early summer afternoon. I was swathed in sunshine, yet I did not feel warm. After being "tossed away" by the minister, rage was pulsing violently through my veins. I had a terrible headache and I found it hard to concentrate on where I was, walking home on automatic pilot. My heart was pounding and my mouth was dry.

I retreated, as fast as I was able, to the "safety" of my home. I went through the back door and straight into the kitchen, pulling open the kitchen drawer beside the stove and pulling out a knife, a very sharp knife. It had a greying wooden handle and a very long blade; my dad often used it to carve roasts. I concealed it in the waistband of my slacks. My anger seemed satisfied that I was preparing for my revenge.

I knew I had to get even with this man. After stealing the knife, I sat down in my bedroom and scrawled out a venomous note, a note of revenge. Still seething, I walked back to the church and placed it on the window of the minister's car. The knife was tucked into the waist of my pants.

For the next two weeks I would write another note every afternoon. "I am watching you. You are going to be dead soon," I warned. Each note was more threatening. I scrawled over and over again that he would die. The knife remained with me every moment, ready to be forced into his uncaring heart. I would feel the knife nicking into my abdomen when I sat down to write. I felt powerful and superior. Yes, I was ready for revenge.

Each day I would return to the church with these death threats, placing them first on his car, then in the mail slot of the church, and slink home in the fading daylight.

There was no response. So at the beginning of the second week, I took the bus to his home. I shoved another threatening note into his mailbox, not knowing it would be my last one.

The minister had been terrified by my notes, afraid to leave his home. His wife feared for her safety as well, as I learned much later. My death threats paralyzed him until he called in the police.

Although he was not sure who was stalking him, the minister had remembered my typed, signed letters seeking his help, still tucked away in his office filing cabinet. Accompanied by the police, he went to the church, found the earlier letters and handed them and the threatening notes to the police. The handwriting was analyzed, and within hours my fate was sealed.

Soon a knock rattled our front door. When my mom answered, two police officers, with voices of concern and authority, told her what I had done. I was no to longer go near the minister, they said, even though he decided not to press charges. I was 17, still a minor.

Just before they left, the officers emphasized that I was not to go anywhere near the church or the minister or I would suffer the consequences of my actions. My devastation was immediate, and the fear of going to prison pushed me into submission.

My plans, once again, would not come to fruition. The minister, the man who rejected me, would be allowed to live. Though I was not happy about this and didn't accept it, I had no choice but to submit.

Days later, the minister called my mom and me into his office. With trepidation, I marched with her into his dark, musty office and sat down. I was fidgeting and uncomfortable. In a forceful and uncaring way, we were told that I was no longer welcome at the church and I was to never come back. My whole church life, from birth until now, flashed before me, and I tried, panicking, to envision a life without my church.

I didn't fully understand the consequences of my actions and could not understand how this banishment from church came about.

My self-harm and suicide attempts had continued through my years at St. John's. At the moment of losing my church, I was more than ever convinced that I had to die.

As I left the church with my mom, I saw, pinned to the bulletin board in the hall, a poster announcing a meeting for parents. It warned of a new, self-destructive behaviour in adolescents, urging all parents to learn more about this. Children were dying, the poster warned. I don't think my mom noticed the poster, but as I was whisked by, I saw it. And then I knew an almost guaranteed way to end my life. My days were finally numbered.

When I got home, I fled to the store at the end of my street. I had abandoned my knife, but pulled money from my pocket and asked for 10 tubes of model airplane glue.

On the way home I plotted the end of my life. Not knowing exactly what to do with the glue, I rustled around in our kitchen drawer and pulled out a plastic bag, filled it with the smelly, sticky substance from several tubes, put it to my face and inhaled deeply. I was transported into a whole new and exciting world. My head became fuzzy at first and then, miraculously, cleared. I felt the power the glue gave me, and I knew I would never be harmed again… not by anyone… mom, dad, Joan, or the teachers or ministers in my life. I would die happy. The tantalization of my ending liberated me, and I sensed, for the first time in my life, a chance for freedom from the chains of earthly living, and the chance to be delivered to the almighty, but angry, presence of God.

I was soon thrust into a deeper pain than I had ever felt before. Right from the moment I started using, I realized I was doomed from ever receiving the love of God in my life. I was devastated.

11 MY ADDICTIONS

In the weeks after I was banned from the church I wallowed in bitterness and rage.

One day I found a copy of the The Satanic Bible in a bookstore. I devoured the pages which carried a new kind of power. If God wouldn't have me, I knew Satan would. Though I never had the guts to follow through on the scary rituals described in the book, I did dream I could. My exploration led me to buy a deck of tarot cards, which my mom grew fond of, and then we bought a ouija board that kept the whole family amused for hours at a time. I learned about pendulums and how they could predict the outcome of anything happening in my life, and I bought one of those.

My first addiction, true addiction, that did not involve any physical self-harm, was to the tarot cards, the ouija board and the pendulum.

I was frozen by the events that had battered me, with no idea what I should be doing. I eagerly used the cards and the pendulum to dictate my next moves in life. I used both many, many times a day, and would not go out or tackle anything without first seeking their advice. I was paralyzed without them.

Even with the cards and other guides, I was afraid to go out of the house, or even to do anything but lie on the floor idolizing the stereo in the living room. I spent most of my time face down on the carpeted floor, spending hours and hours after school and on the weekend. I just drifted into my fantasy world, dreaming of far off places like Ceylon, where I had always wanted to visit. I often just lay down, my mind blank with a kind of life exhaustion, listening to our collection of classical records from the Safeway store.

I became, as I later learned, agoraphobic. I was afraid to go out after dark. Being anywhere but on the floor scared me. Even walking became strange, awkward and clumsy, my breath laboured, my heart pounding irregularly.

I was frightened beyond imagination of what I would do next, and the tarot cards and pendulum gave me a sense of control over my life even as it fell further and further apart. I was hooked on them. The Satanic Bible, which I had taken to hiding under the pillow on my bed, grew less fascinating. I did read, with fascination, newspaper stories about the desecration of Christ Church Cathedral, just up the hill from St. John's, by satanic worshippers. But I really wasn't interested in worshipping Satan, though my relationship with God was very rocky indeed. I finally flung the book into our wood stove in the basement, and latched on to the cards and the pendulum with intensity, knowing I could no longer live my life without them.

Glue, I found, was terribly messy. After squirting a tube or two in my plastic bag and inhaling the fumes, I would emerge from the comfort of the bag over my mouth and nose and find, with horror, that my face was plastered with the clear substance. I looked like my skin was peeling on my cheeks and mouth. I moved into other, less messy ways to get high that still involved "huffing," as it was called by the media.

One day I was in my father's workshop, printing and developing photographs, when I started to rustle around in his spray paint collection on the back wall. With great curiosity I pulled out a spray can of clear lacquer, ran upstairs to get a plastic bag and some Kleenex and fled back downstairs. I squirted the sticky substance — but not as sticky as glue — into the bag and held it up to my face.

A peacefulness overtook me. I suddenly was transported to the lush, green rice paddies of China, saw the workers knee deep in the water and I felt cool and warm all at the same time. I breathed in and out, quickly at first and then, as I sucked in the gentleness of the scene, my breathing slowed down. This was the life.

One day, not long after this 'trip to China,' I filled my Kleenex and bag with more of the lacquer and headed to the basement. As I was walking triumphantly into the space off my dad's workshop, the floor was rent open with great force and a million Satans flew out. My terror caused me to faint; the peacefulness of my huffing was torn from me.

As the days went by, I realized I could no longer live my life without sniffing. I would rush down to the basement every free moment and breathe in the tantalizing, burning smell of the lacquer. I was hooked. When I used, I forgot about dying. Inside though, somewhere, I hoped that I would.

My sister Anne told me years later that she was afraid to bring home school chums after I started sniffing. My anger was intense and, she said, I started packing a knife again and would wield it threateningly in front of her and her friends. My new activity began to change the emotional atmosphere of our home, though I did not see it happening. I had gained some power over everyone.

By this time, my older sister Joan had moved out to attend the BC Institute of Technology in Burnaby, hoping to become a lab technician. Her presence had always felt threatening, and she seemed to have a constant need to harm me. Now there were no more threats from her. And I was, at least theoretically, the big sister, the sibling in charge. I did not take my role seriously, and Anne, more caring and healthier than me, became my emotional mentor and my physical protector. I gave up any right to normalcy and moved further and further into dreamland and addiction.

Home life was just as rocky as it always had been. Mom and dad still fought violently, even though Joan was no longer living there. I was in fantasyland and Anne, in her wisdom, tried to keep the family together.

Somehow, in the end, all her efforts failed.

After I graduated from Victoria High School in 1968 and went on to first year university in the arts and science program, my glue sniffing had become a way of life for me — like putting on my socks and underwear each morning. University life became a total blur and, though I did reasonably well, I dropped out after the first year.

I still wanted to be a nurse, but that dream was doomed. No matter how many times my mom sent out applications to training hospitals, all the applications were returned with rejection letters. Because I had psychiatric help in my earlier years, I did not qualify.

Finally, as a last effort, my mom applied to BCIT for me and, wonder of wonders, I was accepted — a new life had begun.

How unprepared I was to leave home and move away to another city. My fear of losing my huffing source was highest in my worries, as well the loss of a pharmacy to provide my pills — Contac C and aspirin by this time. These fears were stronger than any desire I had to become a nurse. I needed these items more and more. I needed to be able to get them. I no longer was sure that would happen.

12 HOSPITALIZED

I headed off to Burnaby with a large blue Buxton suitcase in hand, escorted by my dad. It was packed with my nursing shoes — tubes of glue tucked carefully into each (I knew it would be easier to conceal tubes of glue rather than tins of lacquer) — and my new nursing outfit, along with other clothes and toiletries. My destination was the home of friends of my parents where I would be staying off and on for a year or so.

My dad spent the whole day with me. We caught an early morning ferry and I met my new house parents, who I knew when they lived in Victoria. Then my dad and I took off for downtown Vancouver to explore some of the sights. My most cherished memory is of going to the matinee at a movie theatre to see Liza Minelli in The Sterile Cuckoo. For once being with my dad was such a pleasure. I was haunted for months by the movie and the feeling of loneliness and desperation that seemed to speak to me. Images from this movie began to pop into my mind uninvited, intruding on my thinking for years to come. Now, after some 50 years, all I can remember is how fast Liza Minnelli spoke in the movie, running verbal rings around her boyfriend as the song "Come Saturday Morning" blasted from the screen. My fantasyland was complete — music, an image, a sadness.

When my dad left for home later in the evening, I hunkered down in my bedroom. I poked a hole into the top of a tube of glue, squeezed it into a plastic bag — also hidden in my shoes — and breathed in the vapours of a new life.

I remember almost nothing of my time at BCIT. Years of electroconvulsive therapy (shock treatment) have erased chunks of my past.

I do know that about three weeks into my course, my dream of becoming a nurse ended abruptly.

I was at my new home cooking dinner. My new house parents — not really my parents, but they seemed like a better substitute — were coming through the blackness from outside at the end of their work days. I was standing by their kitchen stove in the dim evening light as they approached. I placed my hands on the hot burners, all the while staring at them. I suspect I was very high from the glue.

My next memory is of finding myself in the psych ward at the University of British Columbia's Health Sciences Centre — a sterile white room where I would live, off and on, for the rest of that year.

I was forbidden to return to Victoria because of my mom's influence on me. So as I was discharged and re-admitted, I continued staying at my new home through the late fall and early winter. My house parents worked and I was no longer going to school, so I was home all day. Somewhere, somehow, I acquired pills and glue. I was continually stoned and continually taking massive doses of the pills.

The revolving door syndrome began. In the hospital, out of the hospital, in what became the regular and predictable rhythm of my life. Even in the hospital I was still popping Contac C and aspirin in great quantities — I got them at the Westbrook Mall pharmacy, near the Health Sciences Centre.

The hospital was safe for me, and I was free from my family and the life that had shaped me. I quickly fell into the rhythm of ward meetings, therapy groups and, my favourite activity, the ward newspaper. I was in seventh heaven discovering my writing skills, and becoming aware that I had the innate ability to charm others with not only my writing, but with my editing and newspaper skills. I became the head of the ward paper. Life was good.

But constantly being discharged from the hospital and re-admitted eventually became unsettling. When out, I wanted to be in; when in, I wanted to be out. More and more often, I would take the pills, attempting suicide on a regular basis.

My privileges in the hospital became increasingly limited. After a few months, I was no longer allowed to leave the hospital on my own, I had to be escorted by a responsible adult — which usually meant my dad. One day, about six months after I was first admitted, I was told I was being sent to the provincial psychiatric hospital, Riverview (also known as Essondale) because the Health Sciences Centre could no longer handle my continuous, destructive behaviours.

From that moment on that period of my life is a total blur. I know I was admitted to Riverview, housed in the Centre Lawn building, one of 2,600 patients. I had no privileges or freedoms, and was confined to the ward for my year-long stay. For a while I was in a medical straitjacket, my arms strapped behind my back, to prevent me harming myself.

In this strange world, at 18, I made one of my first and closest friends. (I did have one friend in Victoria. When I finally returned home, she had left for Winnipeg).

My new friend's name was Betty. She was witty, funny, creative, with an unusual take on life, and we became instant friends. Although she was younger by a year, we got along as though we had known each other all our lives. Hospital confinement took on a new meaning. I was doing less harm to myself. Betty was the first very bright spot in my life and, when I was to be discharged from Riverview, I urged Betty to follow me. She was slated to be admitted to one of the hospital's back wards as a permanent patient. I did not want that to happen to her, so when I was permitted to return to Victoria, I pleaded with my mom to let Betty stay with us.

My dad had moved out for good by then. In 1970, my parents, in a last ditch effort to save their relationship, holidayed in Japan for Expo '70, the world's fair. My sisters and I were hopeful that this trip would solidify their marriage and bring a wholeness to it. However, when they returned home, sullen and angry, the "D" word was on their lips. My dad moved out almost immediately.

My aunt had been staying with us over the past couple of years, attending Normal School at Camosun College, and she thought having Betty in the house might help my mom heal. The bickering and the emotional abuse continued (the strap and wooden spoons that were a big part of our physical abuse were hidden away). Yet with Betty living with us, both of us fresh from the provincial psych ward, there was a kind of levity to the environment. She was intensely funny and, to my surprise, asked to raise fish. This was my introduction to fish, and my fascination has lasted a lifetime. A tank, sitting on the blocked-in oil tank in the basement, proudly held several piranhas. Hamburger and bugs were all they ate. Betty did the bug hunts; I provided the hamburger. Until my mom realized she could use the fish as a weapon against us.

13 LIFE WITH BETTY

Betty and I both found work that summer. I was working as the executive director's secretary at the YM-YWCA in Victoria, after having completed — with honours — a secretarial course at Sprott Shaw a few months earlier. Betty was working as an aide at Brook Manor, a residence for people with psychiatric issues, miles out of town near Elk Lake.

One evening we returned home to find all our possessions scattered on the front lawn of my mom's place. Bewildered, we both stood looking at the mess and wondered where we would go.

The evening before, I had visited my dad's new duplex on Gladstone Street, a few kilometres away. He had moved around a bit before finally settling on the up/down duplex across from Victoria High School.

He was eager to show off his new home and I went, innocently, to cheer on his prize purchase. That, I fear, triggered my mom's jealousy and feeling of being pushed aside and caused her to react so impulsively against the two of us. The fish tank was on the front lawn, empty. I suspect the piranhas had been flushed down the toilet.

My older sister Joan took me in. She had finished her lab technician course at BCIT a couple of years before and was married, with a house. I camped in her spare room, while Betty found somewhere else to live. But after several months, my dad invited Betty and me to live in the upper part of his duplex. This invitation brought great delight to the both of us. We were soon moving in our paltry possessions.

Betty's mom was moving down from Fort St. John, where she had just retired from the post office, and she also came to live with us.

I have never been as happy as I was during those few years together with this pair. They both loved fun and I, rather a stick in the mud, learned to roll with the almost insane jollity that pervaded our squashed apartment. Their room, under the gable of the upper duplex, was accessible only on hands and knees through a curtained, narrow "doorway." Even inside, the room ceiling was so low you couldn't stand. They often chuckled about having to camp out every night. They seemed happy there, reunited after years of being apart.

The staircase to our apartment chopped our living room in half, and it was so very narrow that only a small chesterfield and coffee table would fit in the area. The kitchen, also quite dinky, was just off the living room. I had a regular bedroom, and there was another room, which I used as a craft area. I never knew why my new friends didn't pick that room to live in, except that I suspect they loved the coziness and adventure of their cramped quarters.

Fun, lots of fun, was the order of the day. We had parties, something I had rarely ever done at home, and had friends camp with us on a blanket on the kitchen floor, eating pork and beans out of tin cans. Hobo Night!

We would dress up in costumes, something else I had never really done, and I went from being a baker with a floppy white hat to Shakespeare with the moustache and short, black jodhpurs to Father Christmas with the long beard, bushy eyebrows and a walking stick, wearing a long, cable knit sweater that I had knit. The sweater was miles too big for me, long and wide, but because I had knit it, I wore it for years and years. Warm it was, but rather ugly. For one party, Betty was Baby New Year with a towel for a diaper. We were always having dress-ups and I loved it. Christmas and Easter were full of joy and presents — stacks and stacks of presents that lurked under our two-foot-high Christmas tree, which took up enough space in the living room to make it hard to get into my bedroom. I didn't care; I was swept along by their excitement.

Having been banned from attending St. John the Divine, I needed a new church. Betty and I wandered just down the street to Metropolitan United Church, where we became friends with the minister, Rev. Laura Butler — a delightful woman with a wonderful sense of life and humour. Her eyes always sparkled in impish fun. She was definitely hard to say "No" to. She introduced us to a close friend of hers, and my sister Anne joined our little group.

We ended up having more parties, even though this was a faith-based group, and each week we had a theme. One time our friend wanted a "pregnancy party" as all of us, the minister included, were single women. The following week, we arrived at this new friend's home with a baby cake and various baby-type presents. She did not answer the door, feebly calling to us to come in. We shuffled excitedly into her den where she was wrapped up in a tartan wool blanket, a floppy ice pack on her head, and her face made up to look as though she could be dying. This costume was so real we could not help but belly laugh at her display. She never dreamed that we would come with gifts and cake, and we all just laughed and laughed that evening. Each week something different happened, and my new life at Metropolitan United Church fulfilled two of my greatest needs — friendship and a liberal faith.

At Metropolitan United, Betty and I volunteered to reinstate their Explorer's program, neither of us knowing what Explorers was. It was similar to Brownies, and the two of us jumped in with both feet and had projects and sleepovers and loads of fun. We met in a room in the newer addition to the church with a window that looked out over a parched, narrow piece of land, squished between the church chapel and the Sunday school wing. Eagerly we took it over, working to make it into a garden. Betty, I and the Explorers were always crawling in and out of the window, giggling and gleefully wielding the hand spades and rakes, making our plot of land a dream come true — for all of us.

I joined the choir as well. It was a top-notch choir with a reputation for excellence. I would often arrive for practice stoned out of my mind, yet I still gloried in the music. Life, though still lived in a haze, was good.

However, when the day ended, and my friends had crawled into their hole in the wall, I would shut my bedroom door, pull out a tin of lacquer thinner and sniff myself to sleep. I am sure the smell pervaded the whole living area, but that never occurred to me then. I needed to keep the high that was constantly in my life, but I never suspected that I was now totally addicted to substance abuse.

The three of us were together for about three years, until the friendships came to a sudden halt when I met and fell in love with a woman my age. I was 22. I spent more and more time with this close friend, sexually active and desperate for the love that flowed between us. We were both "black sheep" in our families and our bonding was strongly formed around our need for safe physical closeness and love. The matter of trust, though we did trust each other innately, was not an issue. Somehow our relationship just filled a hole in both our lives and so trust was not an issue or even thought about, especially by me.

Horrified by this relationship, Betty and her mom moved out. Betty wrote me a scathing letter condemning my life choice, and we did not speak after that for many, many years. I was hurt beyond anything I ever felt at home. Betty died many years later, after a motorcycle crash that resulted in the amputation of one leg. While she was recovering, she was diagnosed with breast cancer, which quickly consumed her. I did not go to her funeral, though I wanted to, because I was still so angry about what had happened many years earlier.

My girlfriend and I continued to live apart. I was still living alone in my dad's duplex and she lived in a tiny apartment five or six blocks away, closer to town. One very hot and humid summer day, after we had been together for seven or eight months, I left her apartment to go to my home. Sometime after I was out the door, she committed suicide.

Not knowing how to process this death, I moved even farther into the black hole that I had left several years before. I was in mourning, guilt-ridden, and ashamed of my sexual choice. I couldn't tell anyone about the loss or my devastation, not until many, many years later.

Her death coloured my view of intimacy and love. I remain celibate even to this day. I shunned people's affections and withdrew into the safe, hazy world of solvent.

My trips to the hospital became increasingly frequent, and for longer and longer periods of time. My self-abuse, not just the solvent use, but the self-inflicted injuries, was more and more vicious, and more frequent. I could not talk to anyone, not even the nurses at the hospital, and I became a recluse, ever more suspicious and afraid.

Because I could only work sporadically since returning home from Riverview, mostly because of my mood swings, self-harm and continuous suicide attempts, I lived on a disability pension from the B.C. government. I rarely went outside anymore, and the fun that had been in my life with my friends died. Life had come to another curve, and the view ahead was totally full of pain and hopelessness.

Nothing has had greater impact in my life than the loss of Betty and her mom and my lover. I stopped caring about my addiction, about the hurt. I became violent towards other people, and this violence was a part of my life almost into my 50s. I did not want to get close to anyone and fought the needs for comforting and nurturing by sniffing myself into oblivion.

People, perhaps hoping to rescue me, perhaps just empathetic, were all around me in my life. I did have friends, wonderful friends, many of whom, one by one, died along the way, but I was numb to their love and their caring.

Now, in my mid-60s, I can let down my guard and let people in. But closeness is still an issue with me, and speaking about my love of someone these days brings me great pain. I feel that by expressing my love, the person will walk away or die and leave me in an emotional turmoil — I could never handle these feelings again. I cannot speak of love or of sexual affinity with someone. I cannot make fun of sexual faux pas like other men and women take great delight in doing. I recognize that I am stuck.

14 DAD REMARRIES

Dad had mellowed quite a bit once he was away from my mom. He was in his 40s now and, though not totally happy about it, worked in the plumbing department of the City of Victoria.

He seemed to thrive in his newly chosen home, the duplex on Gladstone. The idea of remodelling and renovating excited him, as he had always dreamed of being a carpenter. He was a perfectionist, so every detail in converting the duplex into four units was carefully thought out and executed. He was happier than I had ever seen him. In those days he wore an old pair of dress pants and an old polo shirt to work in. Every day he had them washed and ready for the next. Once a smoker, he had taken up the habit again, I think only because there was no mom to harass him into quitting.

He started to hang around the group called Parents Without Partners. I think he went because he was lonely, and somehow latched on to a woman called Beryl. After a short courtship they married on Aug. 3, 1974. I was 24.

Beryl was full of adventure. She had her own car with a short wave radio in it, and she enjoyed rock hounding. Within a few months she had my dad driving the coast of Vancouver Island, Washington and Oregon, looking for specific rock formations and specimens to bring back to Victoria. She was only a few years younger than my dad, but full of the adventuring spirit. Neither my dad nor I had ever even imagined that there was such a wandering way of life. Beryl definitely perked up my dad and he joyfully became her "rock" companion. He had travelled very little, except to work on the west coast of the Island when he was a plumber in my childhood — seasonal work — and now he seemed happy parading around searching for rocks with her.

We had known they were serious, and the marriage was expected. But as the date neared, my mom's threats and rage about the coming wedding held us all hostage. Beryl and my dad were being married in Metropolitan United Church, and my mom kept threatening to show up ,screaming that my dad and potential stepmother had "justified impediments" that should block their marriage. I was so frightened that she would have the nerve to go ahead with this humiliating gesture, and I am sure others were as well. As the wedding progressed, the witnesses and bride and groom kept looking over their shoulders to the back of the church, fearful this mad woman would appear. Mom never showed up, yet I am sure all of us imagined we could hear her high-pitched voice laugh at us from behind the chapel doors.

A honeymoon followed, and the couple returned to Gladstone Street and set up house together. Almost immediately, my stepmom, who also had three sons and two daughters, mostly living in Alberta, began to treat my dad as though he was a little boy, calling him Johnny as she wiped his face after eating. He seemed to like this attention, and it became common to watch her nag, guiding his behaviours as if she were his parent. Dad was happy. Beryl was happy. Their marriage went on with a seeming smoothness that in no way reflected his marriage to my mom.

I was, again, left on the outside. I never did meet all my stepbrothers and stepsisters during the 30-some years that dad and Beryl were married. I believe my parents were ashamed of me; they did not want a substance abuser to be a part of this new family. My sisters Anne and Joan were part of the lives of their new stepbrothers and sisters, but I was left on the periphery. I was never really part of my sisters' lives either.

But it was my doing as well. I was afraid of the huge commitment in becoming part of such a family. I couldn't verbalize my feelings about the changes in our family life or explain my disdain, or pleasure, about the addition of five other members. So I pretended they just did not exist. I did not know how to start developing relationships with them.

That's been true my entire life. I know so little about the friends I have had over the years, afraid to ask in case I was prying. I now feel the loss of the chance to connect, to hear their stories. But I still can't ask today. On the rare occasions I do, I am uncomfortable, thinking I am intruding on their privacy. I think I had, and still do to some degree, lived in my own world for so long that there wasn't room for anyone else by this time. Because I did not volunteer much insight into my life, I felt I could not bond or get to know anyone else. People were to be kept at arms-length. I was shy and always believed (and still do somewhat) that peoples' lives were private, and that they would share their stories with me if they wanted. Most of the time, they never did.

My dad and Beryl, while not drawing me into the larger family, did try to do things with me for a while, until they took me on a trip to Seattle. Hungover and needy, my behaviour put a kibosh on further such excursions. I was never asked to go anywhere with them again.

After about five years in the duplex, I moved out. My living situation was chaotic most of the time. I was moving house many, many times a year in this period, with my sister Anne and dad doing most of the packing and transporting of my belongings to the next, uncertain place. I was on disability assistance from the province, with a subsidy from the Capital Mental Health Association for my housing.

Eventually my dad asked me to be one his tenants again. He had converted the Gladstone duplex to four units, and I was in the suite next to them on the first floor at the back. My stepmom and dad had been married only a few years, and I sensed that my dad felt guilty about my inability to settle into any place. I always believed that he felt somewhat responsible for my mental illness (and perhaps addiction), and this was his way of repenting.

This time, I lived alone. I was lonely, and jealous of my sisters. My bedroom window was near the back door of my dad's place. I would hear my sisters arriving at his door for a party or dinner. And I was rarely invited.

I would sniff more and more on those evenings.

My addiction had caused a huge chasm in my family relationships. I also suspect that dad really did not know me very well — that I was a crazy family appendage that needed to be overlooked. I was hurting and, rather than being able to give up my huffing, I did more and more of it. I had no skills to express my feelings, no confidence or assertiveness.

I made one or two late night forages in my dad's basement workshop, prying open his paint cupboard and helping myself to some spray lacquer. It did not take him long to realize that I was stealing from him, and he wasted no time bolting the door shut. My behaviour, fuelled by the overwhelming need to use, started to break down any morals I had. I was living moment to moment in survival mode. I could let nothing get in my way.

Over the years of my dad's remarriage, he — sometimes with Beryl — often rescued me from heavy using to feed me. He would almost drag me from whatever apartment I was currently living in and load me into their car. They took me to restaurants and drive-ins for food to feed my often neglected belly. Often he would require me to give him a kiss on the lips, which I still hated. And then they would drop me back home to continue with my sniffing. I had no shame, just a withdrawal hangover.

I really did want to be left alone; my social skills were almost nil. I was a loner from a long way back, and I did not know how to interact with my two sisters either. I often played the clown when I was with them until I drove everyone, my dad included, so crazy that they would plead for me to stop this insane game. Of course, I would not stop, and kept on until everyone walked away.

When my father died on March 12, 2006, I met all of Beryl's family at his Celebration of Life. He and Beryl had been married for more than 30 years, and I realized I had only been in their condo, which they had moved to from the Gladstone house years earlier, about three times — once when my dad had taken ill when he was in his 80s and I invited myself. I felt banned and abandoned. I felt I was a source of shame and a source of anger. I am sure my dad just did not want me to exist within his almost perfect new family, particularly since I was often intoxicated and on a manic high.

Beryl died a few years later. My dad, in his will, left me a small trust fund that was intended to keep a roof over my head and food in my belly. To this day, the trust fund does just that. I didn't realize my dad truly did care about my plight in life — mental illness and addiction. Yet he took pains to make sure that those things that were often too hard for me to manage would be looked after.

I now have an appreciation of my dad that I was afraid to even acknowledge when he was alive. He scared me then. It was always his eyes that I saw as devil's eyes, that still turned me away from knowing or trusting him.

My mom? She had died years earlier on Dec. 16, 1982. I was never close to her and had little contact after my dad's wedding. Because of my using and the electroshock therapy I cannot remember her funeral at all. I believe I attended, but cannot say for sure.

15 LOST IN ADDICTION

As my addiction took over, I faced major changes in my life.

It's hard to write about the period, because so much of it is a blur. Some time after my stay in the UBC Health Sciences Centre in the late 1960s, I ended up committed to Agape House, a mental health boarding home run by a retired nurse who was also looking after her elderly mother on site. I spent more than a year there. I had been in the hospital much too much, and my family was not keen on having me live with them. I was, admittedly, a disruptive presence.

I bounced in and out of a series of apartments, other housing arrangements and hospital over the next several years.

During this time, I lived in many unsavoury rooms and places on the brink of being demolished, dotted around Victoria. I typically just stayed in most of them for a few weeks, maybe a little longer, before I was hauled off to the psych ward at the Eric Martin Pavilion at the Royal Jubilee Hospital. I often left others, to the anger of my sister Anne and dad, to pack up, throw out and clean up my apartments that I left behind.

Why they did this for years and years and years I do not know. I do know that they won't ever do that again. My dad has died, and I know Anne will no longer help clear out my belongings from any apartment I live in these days. And I can't blame her.

I ended up in my second mental health boarding home after another hospitalization due to an attempted suicide. I believe my admissions to the Eric Martin Pavilion, a newly opened psychiatric facility that was part of Royal Jubilee Hospital, were becoming too frequent, and in an effort to stop the revolving door syndrome the psychiatrist had me placed — or rather committed — to English Manor, a psychiatric boarding home on Point Street, just a block from the ocean in Fairfield. The old, narrow home looked like it had been plucked from England. It was run by Yvonne Andrews, a tiny East Indian lady of boundless energy and an often curt tongue. My roommate, a chain smoker who never moved off her bed, annoyed me right from the beginning. Not wanting to be in this prison of a home, I antagonized my roommate as much as I could, often throwing pillows and other things at her, yelling at the top of my lungs, "Do something!"

I was not the most popular patient at this psychiatric boarding home. Many years later, I returned to the manor with a potential client who was participating in a program I was running. The same cook — Deep — still worked there, and had an immediate question.

"Do you still hit people?"

Yvonne took pity on me, perhaps because I was the youngest client there, about 24 or 25. She owned property in various parts of the city and would often take me to work for her. I would paint, hang wallpaper, scrub floors, hammer nails into whatever needed a nail. She paid me with clothes and often a meal out. I suppose feeling comfortable that I would behave, she then began taking me to church. Not knowing my previous histories with churches, she could not know how this venture would turn out.

On the first Sunday, dressed in my best blue jeans and hunter's fleece shirt — both men's wear from the local Capital Iron store on Store Street — we drove off to the Church of Our Lord, which was not far from the legislature buildings. Yvonne introduced me to the congregation, most dressed in their Sunday best. Many people, curious about this blue-jeaned, flannel-shirted woman, came up to inspect me the first day. Though I felt embarrassed by my garb sometimes, I did not choose to change my wardrobe until a couple of years later.

At first I wasn't impressed by this church. It was Reformed Episcopalian, Anglican, of sorts, but had a different feel to it — a little more fire and brimstone than my memories of St. John the Divine. However, for about five or six years after that, I darkened the door of the church each Sunday, with Yvonne running behind me to make sure I behaved appropriately.

To this day I have two of my most wonderful friends who were from that time. Claudia, the minister Charles Dorrington's wife, and Joan Smith, a member of the choir, which I finally joined after a couple of years. I sang in the rather professional choir, cheerfully supported by the choir director Charles, who had the voice of an angel. I stuck with it, singing anthems and hymns at Thursday evening choir practices and Sunday morning services at eleven.

Today I count my blessings for the time I was able to spend with this choir, and for meeting these two women who continued to journey with me, unconditionally and with love, all these years. Though we are all getting older now and have various health issues, we still remain friends to this day.

Although my residence had changed with the move to English Manor, I was still an addict. In the middle of the night I would sneak down the stairs of the manor, lacquer thinner and a plastic bag and Kleenex under my arm, unlock the front door and head for the beach. The manor was near Clover Point and the ocean.

Down on the beach I would huff my head into a more pleasant world. However, more often than not, the police arrived shortly after and hauled me off to jail to sober up for the night. My hope was that Yvonne would cast me out of the manor. She never did. I now know this was because I was committed there under the Mental Health Act and I needed to be discharged by my psychiatrist.

Toward the end of my stay at the Manor I looked after a very old lady, bedridden and residing in the downstairs dining room. I would toilet her, enchant her with my stories, and often change her gown. Because she was in the dining room, we all, about 10 of us, ate in the living room, a narrow, furniture-cluttered place that revolved around the TV. Living room meals meant TV trays that were put up and taken down three times a day — annoying, but part of our daily routine. None us wanted to miss a meal because Deep, our cook, chugged out the most wonderful food, and we lived only to eat, most of us at least.

Finally, considered more stable after about four or five years, I left English Manor, regally saying my goodbyes to all the old regulars, and moved back into my dad's home.

My dad felt it would be easier to keep an eye on me if I lived at his place again, in an apartment on the lower floor of the fourplex. I think he hoped I would stop using. The reality was I could not stop.

Through the late '70s and early '80s I lived at my dad's place for extended periods. First in the duplex, until I was evicted while he fastidiously converted the building into a fourplex.

As my hospitalizations increased, the therapies became more and more insane — sleep therapy, primal scream, bioenergetics, electroconvulsive therapy. I would leave each stay with a new plan to manage my mental health. But I had no intention of managing my mental health. The reality was, I couldn't. I lived to get stoned, mostly in an effort to keep the ever-increasing demons in my head away. During all of this time — and before and after — I struggled with vicious and intrusive thoughts that I could not shake or push away.

Often, while under the influence, I would make attempts on my life. I was truly miserable. Friends and family may have been around, but I continued to feel totally alone. I was becoming more and more withdrawn and out of tune with the social wiles and niceties that governed daily life.

I tried to hold a job, but I just couldn't. With my addiction and my mental state, I could not comprehend the idea of a nine-to-five work day, or the constant workplace commands and demands. In the end I just settled on volunteering.

With volunteer jobs, I found I could go, protected by solvent whiffed an hour earlier, and the staff were still nice to me, not critical nor demanding. I worked for a few years with a most wonderful woman, Jean Mosley, at the Canadian Diabetes Association, crammed into a storefront on Pandora Street, just across the street from Metropolitan United Church (now known as First Metropolitan United). She would often take me home for supper or out to a movie. She gently took me under her wing. I worked very hard at the association. I didn't spend much time in the office, but there was also a hub of activity in a large back room, where I worked happily several days a week. Every day I handled paper, more paper and the utmost piles of paper, photocopied, collated and distributed to clients who had diabetes and their families. Even though I was in the back, generally away from the public, I often found myself greeting the customers. I worked hard at being kind with the public, and I was interested and full of vigour.

I loved this job. But then Jean died of a heart attack. I was sent into a tailspin of mourning. The association moved its office and I returned to the invisible background of life after leaving this volunteer position. I ended up back in the hospital, as I so often did after changes in my life.

My next important volunteer job was, believe it or not, back at St. John's Church. The minister, Rev. Canon Robert MacCrae, took me under his wing to help with his pet project, a campaign to stop Nestlé from promoting the use of infant formula in developing countries. The name of our program was INFACT CANADA. I became a researcher and a gopher. I liked both aspects of the job, and I also liked being allowed back at St. John's. I was home again, and all the terror I had caused in the past seemed to have blown over.

I do not know how long I worked with INFACT, but I eventually moved on.

And yes, once again, I would arrive at work totally stoned. I could never seem to muster confidence to do a task if I wasn't full of the gas from lacquer thinner. I did not believe that I was good for anything or anybody. And as much as many people tried to change my internal image of myself, I never believed them — not for years and years and years.

16 I BECOME A TEACHER

One day, rather suddenly, I developed a great determination to right my life's path. It was about 1976. I was 26 and had nothing to show for my life but a dumpster full of empty lacquer thinner cans and a long history of violence towards myself and others. These long periods were salted with depression for which I received little help — yet how could a psychiatrist really diagnose me anyway? I was stoned most of the time.

I don't know why, but I decided to become an early childhood education teacher and enrolled in Camosun College in the late 1970s. With trepidation and excitement, I knuckled down to my studies. I was already an avid reader and could digest at least seven books a week, not just novels but non-fiction. Stoned or not, I could still read and retain the essence of the books for fairly long periods of time. Studying was easier this time — not like the confusing drudgery I vaguely remembered from university. I loved the courses and I loved the instructors — Nora Lupton, Larry Dettweiler and others. Eager to do well and be accepted, I brazenly nuzzled up to the professors, lapping up their praise. I excelled in the courses, maintaining an A average.

During the two years in this course I practised harm reduction in my solvent use and was quite successful with this technique, even though I did not recognize it as a way to manage addiction until much later in my using career. Somehow, I learned to use only on weekends while white-knuckling my sober days during the week.

Because my life was totally focused on doing well in school, I never really thought ahead about the reality of my future once the course had ended. My goal was to become a pre-school teacher, even though it was not fully accepted as a profession in those days.

For the first time in my life, or at least I felt it was the first time, I accomplished one of my goals: to start and complete a program and then return to the work force. My dad, so proud of me and filled with hope for my future, perched himself in the college auditorium on my graduation day, watching me walk across the stage to receive my diploma. Though I was anxious and awkward during the ceremony, I had achieved success, graduating with honours in April 1978. I was now a qualified preschool teacher.

However, there was a problem. During the two years I was at Camosun College, I truly never gave any thought to the idea that I would be working with actual children. Even though I was studying child development and psychology, and had a practicum at a day care centre before graduation, I'd never thought much about actually teaching in a centre — I just wanted to be qualified as a teacher and excel at my studies, and I accomplished both. My lack of planning now seems absurd to me.

Then came my first position at a day care centre downtown near what was then the Eaton's Centre. The shock of standing in front of real live children came upon me right from day one. I was awkward and afraid of these youngsters, and I knew it — and I was sure they knew it too. I just wasn't prepared to be on the front lines.

My excitement and confidence started to slide. I began forgetting about harm reduction and looking after my mental health. I know that I was an asset to the centre, despite my self-doubts, yet shortly after my first position I began moving around between day cares, looking for that golden position. In between jobs — and sometimes while working — I would end up in the hospital, suicidal, totally depressed and often stoned.

Almost 40 years later, I still view my teaching days as a total failure, even though I worked at some of the best day cares in the city.

After about two years I dropped out of the work world once again. Stress was the biggest factor in my departure, as it was in all the positions I left before this. I couldn't handle interacting with my workmates and, in this case, with the children. I was so shy and lacking self-confidence that I felt like I was a living secret-holder and that everything I did was being watched and judged. These thoughts became my life once again. Hospital visits were increasing, and so were suicide attempts and other self- destructive behaviours.

I started on a downward spiral that, almost a decade later, would bring me to my knees, humiliated and shattered beyond anything I could ever have imagined. I was doomed for more and more failures and, once again, I withdrew into the safety of my own world.

17 MY THIRTIES: LOST FRIENDS, LOST YEARS

I sit at my desk, nestled in my bedroom, under a western window that lets in some light. It's October 2016. I am thinking about what I've learned and observed as I write this book. My 66th birthday is in two weeks. The more I write, the more I begin to remember small details of my life, and the people I've known. I cannot help but believe that God has a hand in my ability to remember details in my life, for I had pushed the past away, into a deep, deep place in my psyche. She gently lifted these memories from that quite dark place into my current consciousness. I do know my memories are true and real, because I can see the people and places with great vividness in my mind.

Up until now, I had no reason to remember people. Memories hung randomly in the gallows of my mind. I didn't want to remember people like the gentle and caring couple, Peggy and John Mika, who often had me over to their home for weekend retreats so I could wander through their Japanese gardens and walk the beaches of Cordova Bay. After much frustration with my inability to grow and appreciate their surroundings and their hospitality, I presume, they moved on in their life without me.

I was a hardcore addict, self-absorbed and unreliable by the early 1980s. A counsellor, Patricia Humphrey, tried her utmost to whip me into becoming a "normal human being" again — if I ever had been — by walking the beach with me near her home on Lands End Road and talking with me week after week. She was attempting to get me to talk about and accept my life path as a lesbian. However, I wanted none of that. Being a lesbian was not exactly what I wanted, and the memories of my first and only love hurt too much to dredge them up for healing. Though I always enjoyed the beautiful surroundings and Pat's charming company, I could never seem to get the hang of what "getting well" meant, so I would quickly slip back into my usual habits once I left her place.

My visits with Patricia were often preceded by a stay with my wonderful friends Belle and John Harrison and John's mom on Tanner Road in Central Saanich. On Friday afternoons I would bus to their place and spend the weekend, visiting markets and driving down country roads, sharing meals in their warmly decorated home. Early Monday morning I would take the bus from their place to meet up with Pat, who would pick me up at the bus stop. I was often too early for my meeting with her, and poked happily along the magical, forested road. Pat, too, disappeared into the fog that clung to the shore, and I moved on to other people.

Friends were easy to come by in those days, but not easy for me to keep. I seemed almost clueless about what friendship truly was. I was so used to people coming and going in my life that losing friend after friend seemed almost to be normal.

I was still couch-hopping. People from my church and other churches would take me in as a tenant. I was given a free room and meals with the expectation that I would help with the chores. Try as I might to stay sober, I couldn't seem to. So after a week or two I would be shipped out to someone else's place with the hope that they might have the magic wand to redeem me from my way of life. This transformation never seemed to happen, and all these friends were lost.

I am not sure how I got caught up in this web of people entering and leaving my life, offering me their homes only to ask me to move on a while later. I do not know how or who orchestrated these living arrangements. All I do know now is that I was a most unwelcome guest and not easily rehabilitated. All of these friends seemed to reach the same conclusion. Either I did not care or I did not know how much angst I had caused everyone. I seemed to think that it was normal for some people to live the way I did.

Still, people wanted to change me. Especially religious people.

I encountered "Father John" when I started attending Christ Church Cathedral, a rather grand, high Anglican church, as I continued my search for a spiritual home. I don't know why, but I was always driven to get to know at least one of the ministers from every church I attended. I wanted approval by God's agents so much that I would write letters to the chosen ministers and meet up with them soon after I began attending their churches. I hoped the minister would take me under his or her wing and transform me into a solid churchgoer and person of faith.

But Father John left me with the impression that Christians simply did not huff. And so, after another unsuccessful effort to make me a strong person of faith and a rehabilitated addict, I left the church once again after Father John advised me that I perhaps need not go to church at all.

I took his advice, for a long, long time. I was relieved to do so. Somehow, even in the world of Christianity, I could not fit in. I wasn't a wholesome, tithe-paying, conforming and a working individual. In fact, I was often told by these Christian folk that I was just not acceptable to God.

One time during my couch-surfing I stayed with a young married pastor and his wife and their three young children. They tried and tried to rehabilitate me. I remember sitting alone, in the dark, on my bed in the basement bedroom. A bit of light scratched through the small window high in the wall, but it was never comforting. I would cry, rocking back and forth in loneliness. Paralyzed with fear and hopelessness.

So I turned to huffing once again. And was thrown out on my ear after yet another very short time.

No one seemed to realize that a lonely bed in a grim, cold room would send me looking for a can of lacquer thinner.

People took me on as a project and took me into their homes, bless their souls, but I never sensed they were doing this babysitting job out of compassion. They were looking to take pride in trying to "transform" me. I wasn't a person; I was part of some quest.

I couldn't respond to their titanic efforts. They all wanted me to stop sniffing. I couldn't, not on their timetable. It was a huge part of my life and my lifestyle. I did not know any other way to live. I suppose these people modelled different ways of dealing with life's challenges. But no one actually took the time to teach me new life skills, new ways of thinking and new ways of communicating.

It's different now. I've attended drug and alcohol treatment programs, as well as one-to-one counselling, sporadically for years. I was always greeted without expectations. I knew I wasn't expected to become sober in one fell swoop. I had been addicted too, too long. I had to train my mind and body to develop basic living skills I never learned at home. I also had to learn self-compassion.

This was the most humongous skill for me to learn, and it wasn't until I was almost 66 that I first caught a glimpse what this self-compassion could look like. In the past, during times of mania, I would push myself into states of exhaustion by my flighty and fast living. In times of depression, which always seemed to follow the mania, I would sit, isolated, huffing to escape the pain of failure. But through the gentle and loving care of the addiction counsellors and a case manager, I learned to slow down a little, taking in deep breaths of calm and quieter activities. By the mid 2000s, I began to believe I could sustain some semblance of calm in times of highs and lows. I knew I needed to do this for safety reasons, yet I struggled to avoid the deep depressions that came with this calming space.

I knew I needed to stop using and face my pain and mental torment. And I did.

Yet even as I write this book, I am still very much suicidal in my thoughts. The depressions still come with a certain regularity, while the mania, controlled mostly by medications, has been curtailed for the most part. And today, in 2016, I am sober. I am successfully learning centering — without solvent. Though this has been a very hard journey, I am able to do it using tools like Word Find puzzles, connect-the-dots exercises and colouring as ways to focus my mind on inner peace, along with the constant and important use of prayer to bring me closer to the God that has kept her hand on me throughout my journeying. Mindful exercises from cognitive behaviour therapy groups along the way also seemed to help in this process. I fought the quiet places, because they did not seem to be as fun as manic highs. And I fought to keep my highs, until I realized that the lows, which I hated, always followed.

"Why do I need to do this calming down?" I asked myself, until I found the answer — for peace.

It took me years and years to develop, even a little, the ability to accept myself. In fact, it was only after about 44 years of using, up until my 62nd birthday, that I achieved total sobriety.

Before I actually sobered up, I spent a long time trying to manage my use with harm reduction tactics, limiting the times or places or amounts I would use. It didn't work, especially since each time I "fell off the wagon," I would sniff myself into oblivion and abandon the cutting-back tactics that came with harm reduction.

I also could not distract myself by doing other things rather than focusing on getting high. The more I thought I distracted myself with things like walking and knitting, the more I wanted to use. The cravings never seemed to be stifled.

I attended detox a few times, but these trips were unsuccessful because of my mental illness. I could not be taken off all my medications, which the detox staff did, and find health. I would cry and scream in suicidal torment the five days I stayed there each time. Eventually I was banned from using these services because I was a disruption to those men and women taking the detox program seriously.

Talk therapy in out-patient addiction groups failed miserably because I had great difficulty, even then, talking about those things that got in the way of my sobriety — family problems, sexual preferences, anger, loneliness and other feelings.

I still did harm to myself and didn't really reduce my chemical use, so finally I had to concede that complete abstinence was the only solution for me. I did not even really try seriously to be sober until around 2005.

Becoming determined to find a civilized way of life — that is, not using — I chose to finally have a go at cleaning up "cold turkey." I did this by using skills I had inadvertently picked up at the alcohol and drug programs. I had in the past tried Alcoholics Anonymous and Narcotic Anonymous groups to gain sobriety, but even in those programs I failed drastically. This time, I decided I just had to stop — and I finally succeeded in gaining sobriety in March 2012. I have not had to look back since then. Now I am proud that I have been victorious over my solvent use.

Why I have kept hammering down the door of churches throughout my life, I truly do not know. I suppose I wanted to be accepted by someone, and thought God might then overlook my flaws. Unfortunately, in my mind the treatment I received from some Christians and clergy came to represent God's attitude toward me. Many wonderful people tried to help me make the changes that would allow me to fully engage with society, but most of them usually just gave up after a while. I can't blame them. But I wondered if God had also given up on me.

I still tried to gain acceptance in this spiritual world. But I was fighting the feeling people saw me as a "second class citizen." Most church people seemed much better off financially, many held important positions. I, on the other hand, seemed not able to work most of the time, partly due to my bipolar illness (which was running rampant at this time), but also because of my disabling addiction.

I felt I would never fit in. I never seemed to fit in with my family nor with my friends. Most of all, I never seemed to fit in with any of my churches. From childhood, I felt I was an outcast and a failure.

I walked close to the edge of death those years. I continued to convince myself that I was unworthy to have a place on this the earth, especially among "good Christian" people. I find this so utterly ridiculous now, as there was no end of good Christian people flooding through my life.

But in the early 1980s — the start of my third decade — my self-image plummeted to a place where it almost did not exist at all. My loneliness and intense confusion about my life led me to become a liar and a fantasizer. I could no longer tell right from wrong; good from bad; truth from lies.

In my fantasy world I was powerful, making everyone I ruled over bow down to me and idolize me. And, increasingly, I couldn't tell if I was living in the real world or my fantasy creation. They were both real.

My fantasies put me in dangerous places, and I was not able to see the consequences of what I was doing and saying. Life seemed hopeless and isolating.

And I raised the ante without really being aware that I had.

18 PRISON

As I descended into despair and delusion, my younger sister Anne gave birth to sons in 1984 and 1987 — my nephews. At first their arrival offered a sense of comfort to me as I tried — unsuccessfully — to sort out my life. I was living at my father's place once again, in the newly finished downstairs unit in the fourplex. I was not working as my mental illness had progressed so much so that I couldn't. My sniffing had progressed too, moving from terrible to worse. My hospitalizations were frequent and often long. My suicidal thoughts and self-harm were a constant part of my life. When I was in the hospital I felt safe, but when I was out in the community, as an out-patient of the Mental Health Centre, I felt scared, and often angry at myself and my world.

The appearance of these two new folk made me feel I was in competition for my sister's love. Anne had become like a mother to me long before our mother's death in 1976, providing a sense of security and love that I had not known from our mother. Anne pampered me, knowing that my mental health issues bothered me. She would listen when I talked about them. She took me under her wing and helped with shopping as well as laundry. Often she would cook meals for me to share with her and her young family, giving me food to take home. As I did not cook much for myself and was often very, very hungry, I relied on this gesture to relieve the pangs I often felt.

I did not know how to love a baby or a child, never having had the opportunity to learn. Babies, for me, were created from acts of brutality in the bedroom and I wanted no part of the end result.

I seemed to invade my oldest nephew's territory more than his younger brother. Once, when he was just a few months old, I was caught shaking him, and was forbidden to hold him after that. His crying disturbed me and I could not understand the noise he made and felt helpless to stop it. There was little chance for bonding or auntie love, and the gap has never really been closed.

Life with my nephew became a constant nightmare. I was afraid of him, or rather afraid of what I might do to him. My sister had me over often during this time. Understanding how she justified letting me near my nephew after the shaking incident, even though he was now older, has always puzzled me. Nonetheless, she did let me do my "auntie" bit.

I had discovered I was afraid of children after I had studied early childhood education, though I could not identify where my fear came from. I was awkward around them, and my nephew was no different.

When Anne's oldest son was around four or five years old, I began to think — and tell others — that I was improper with him. I was so upset by my sister's focus on her children and her lost affection that I never really stopped to think what was actually happening. My mind began playing tricks on me and, gloatingly, I was telling certain people that I was having my way with this male child.

One day, at a psychologist's appointment, I broached the subject and said perhaps I was molesting my nephew. Without hesitation, she picked up the telephone and called the police. In that moment I was thrown into a confusion that has never left me. I am not sure today whether I did harm my nephew. I just don't know.

The police came to my home a day or two later and told me I was forbidden to be around my sister and her family, or any other family members except for my father. I was also given an order to appear in court within two weeks.

My older sister, Joan, was graduating with a bachelor of science degree from the University of Victoria and I had been invited to the ceremony. At the last moment, I had to tell her that I could not come. I realized years later that she did not know about the "no contact" order imposed by the police and was hurt and angry that I had bowed out of the commitment, anger she carried throughout the rest of her life. I'm convinced this was the beginning of a huge rift between Joan and me; it took years and years before we could even begin healing the wound, and even now it still exists.

On the day of Joan's graduation, my dad tried to make me feel a part of this moment, bringing a piece of her graduation cake back to me in the fourplex. I cried and cried at being banned from sharing the day with her.

I felt so alone and lost in the midst of my legal crisis, and I could no longer rely on Anne for her mothering love. I seemed to have lost everything that was valuable to me.

Within a few weeks I found myself standing alone in court before a judge. The lawyer I had was from Legal Aid, provided by the court. Scared and confused, I listened to the count against me — sexual interference with a minor. I was remanded for two more weeks. I could not believe what was happening to me; I could not believe how my imagination had got me into so much trouble. For a year, I appeared back in court every two weeks. Toward the end of that time, the minister of Church of Our Lord offered to provide support and love by standing with me. No one else had, not even my dad.

As the weeks progressed, I was never sure what I had actually done — or not done — to my nephew. My brain told me one thing, my body told me another. I was desperate for love during this time — sexual and emotional. As I was not involved in any relationships, I did not know what to do with the disturbing and ever increasing sexual feelings. Around this time my genitals started to throb and hurt terribly. I was ashamed at what my body was doing and tried to cover it up.

So with my nephew, I did not know what was the truth — was I using him to relieve the pressure, or was I just confused and intimidated by my body's feelings?

In the end I attempted suicide, and ended up, once again, in the psychiatric unit of the Eric Martin Pavilion in Victoria under the watchful eye of a one-to-one nurse. The night before I was to be in court for the last time, I was harassed by the psychiatrist on duty and my anger swelled to horrendous proportions. My suicidal thoughts were almost unbearable.

In court the following day I was ordered to have a 30-day psychiatric review at the psychiatric prison, Colony Farm, across the highway from Riverview in Port Coquitlam.

My dad, who questioned the order, accompanied me to the prison. By this time, I was numb, yet in the dark recesses of my consciousness I knew I would ultimately kill myself. I felt so dirty and so defiled that I could not imagine anyone caring about me ever again. I went to the prison willingly, wanting to be punished for my indiscretions — and no amount of punishment would be enough to redeem my horrendous acts, real or imagined.

From the moment my dad and I arrived at Colony Farm, my life was changed forever. Still not sure I had committed a crime, I was stripped of my clothes, roughly searched in all orifices and finally thrown into a tub of very hot water. Two women staff scrubbed my body until it almost bled and scratched at my hair until it almost fell out. Standing naked in front of these women, who seemed to like their dominant role, I could not hide my shame any longer and broke down crying. They just laughed and ordered me to get dressed in pajamas. Shaking and crying, I found it difficult to get dressed.

Once I had, the two guards gruffly led me down a long corridor to a room where other inmates were having dinner. No tables, just TV trays, as they were sharing the men's quarters because renovations were being made to the women's section, so there was no dining room for the women. The inmates were joking with each other, but I was so scared and had no appetite. The women, showing off, I suspected later, were telling grisly stories of burning down buildings or stabbing their husbands, gloating and boasting of crimes they had committed.

I was horrified by their candour and their levity. How could I live with people like this? What would they do to me if they found out why I was there? On TV I had seen many stories about men who had committed sexual offences who were bullied and violently assaulted — even brutally killed — by their fellow inmates. I feared for my life. I could not speak.

I had not been in this community room for more than a half hour when a guard tapped me on the shoulder and asked me to follow. He was an office worker, I learned, not a regular guard — the front line staff were on strike. I was quietly ushered to a cell that had only a mattress on the floor, draped with a couple of sheets and a pillow. On the mattress sat a man who, I later was told, was from the administration. He gently asked me to sit down. Though I was so very frightened, I did. But then, probably because I was so scared, I started banging my head on the concrete wall. I felt I was in a dream that was full of horror and venom. I just wanted to die.

That's why I was in this cell — the staff knew I was a suicide risk.

For almost a week, I was watched around the clock by at least one staff person who either sat in the cell or lingered just outside the door to give me a chance to sleep. The men were gentle; the women were not as polite. The women administrators seemed restless when they sat with me and indicated, through their stiff demeanour, that they did not want to be there.

Prison life made my shame unbearable. Not only was I walked to washrooms with six bulky men who watched while I urinated, I was also watched in the shower as I scrubbed myself down. I had absolutely no privacy and, as I was to find out, I never would in prison.

After 30 days I was shackled, hands and feet, and packed into an RCMP paddy wagon along with a couple of other inmates, separated from the driver and guard by a wire cage. The three of us were driven to the Vancouver airport to an isolated hanger. My 30-day assessment was up so I was returning to court. I had never flown, and was frightened at the prospect. I struggled to get into the four-seat plane with the shackles on, fearing a fall to the pavement. I could not lift my leg high enough to clear the door jam, and the impatient guard accompanying us threw a few curse words my way. By the grace of God, I was finally able to enter and sit down. The plane seemed small and I wondered about my safety — a strange thing, as I still really just wanted to die.

Once in Victoria, I was forced into another caged vehicle, with many, many cages in it and many, many men. Each cage had a small, narrow wooden seat — very narrow! Going around corners was terrifying because all I had to hold onto was the cage's chicken wire. I was not eager to land on my face in front of all those desperate-looking men.

I was in the cage closest to the back doors, the only woman. I road uncomfortably to the courthouse, with a stop at the Wilkinson Road provincial prison to pick up a few more passengers

At our destination, the Court House across from Christ Church Cathedral, the guard took me down to a small cell somewhere in the basement. The lawyer who was to handle my case showed up. This, once again, was the lawyer I had during my court appearances 30 days before — he was still associated with Legal Aid. He quickly interviewed me, but asked few questions and seemed to have no concern about my interests. He hadn't studied the psychiatric report from Colony Farm, he said, before telling me what to say in court.

After an hour or two in the small, cold cell, I was escorted to the courtroom by a female guard. I have no idea whether I pleaded guilty. My lawyer spoke, the judge's gavel hit the desk and he declared I would be sent back to Colony Farms for an unspecified length of time.

Once again, I was to be accompanied by my father. But it was Friday afternoon, and no one would be at the prison to receive me until Monday morning, so the court commanded that I take a room at a local motel, specified by them, and wait to travel back to the mainland on the Monday.

After my dad dropped me off at the motel I was relieved to be alone for the first time in months. I left my room once that weekend. Late that night I took the little money I had been given for food and went to the nearby Canadian Tire and bought a tin of lacquer thinner. I never left my room for the remainder of the weekend.

The days were humid and very hot. The hotel room was sweltering. However, once I opened my tin of solvent, I huffed until I no longer cared what was happening in my world. The whole weekend I lay on the top of the bedcovers and didn't eat or drink until my father came to pick me up early Monday morning. The ferry trip back to Vancouver was full of dread about returning to Colony Farm, yet back I went. On the ferry I felt so sick to my stomach as I withdrew from my weekend of huffing and no food. I felt like I could have died. However, when we arrived at the prison office, I was, once again, led back to a separate cell where I stayed for almost the rest of my sentence.

19 TURNING FORTY IN JAIL

About four weeks into my sentence the guards' strike ended and they came back to work, while the administrative staff went back to their regular tasks.

Women guards began sitting with me, holding my head tightly at times to prevent me from banging it against the wall. One guard, in particular, took to hugging me close to her — at least until she found out I was a lesbian. Stupidly and regrettably, I told her. At that moment she pushed me away, stood up and walked out of the room. She wore a distinctive perfume that lingered behind. I never set eyes on her again.

From that moment on, no one came to see me. I was locked in a small, cold cell that had a barred window high on the wall that was never closed. There was only me, in my pajamas, and a plastic-covered mattress with no bedding. The grey metal door had a small window, usually covered with a thin wooden panel. Guards could slide it open to see what I was doing, and a convex mirror high up in a corner of the cell let them see the entire space. I was alone and afraid, and spent almost the entire time I was in prison in my cell, curled up in a fetal position, mostly to stay warm, but also to fall in and out of a tortured sleep. My food tray was shoved under the door, and when I needed to go to the bathroom I would have to bang on the door, sometimes for what seemed like hours, to get the six burly men to take me. A few times, needing to pee so badly, I just did it in the corner of the cell when no one would answer my frantic knocks. Humiliation and degradation.

The psychiatrist responsible for the unit took me into his office one day to do psychiatric testing. I was so relieved to be out of the cell that I talked non-stop while eagerly doing the written and visual tests.

In the end, much to my horror, I found out I had been labelled "Borderline Personality Disorder." The tiny amount of my remaining self-respect was stripped from me. I had never heard this label, before but the results of it caused the psychiatrist to advise the staff that no one was to speak to me — ever.

In those days, the label was like a death sentence, considered untreatable and the lowest of low psychiatric disorders. People with Borderline Personality Disorder were seen as attention seekers, suicidal, acting out with no sense of shame and totally self-absorbed. With this label, I became more isolated. I was mentally abused by the staff — they were forbidden to talk to me, so I spent almost my whole time in prison with no verbal exchanges. I was also shunned by the other inmates the rare times I was let out of my cell.

One day, I reached out with kindness to a woman who, when I was out of the cell, shared the prison ward with me. I had offered to protect her from the staff one morning as she was finding it difficult to wake up and get out of bed. She responded to my gesture by telling the staff stories about me and how I was mistreating her. Her venomous rage destroyed what little chance I had of human contact. I was immediately returned to my cell after being chastised by the staff for verbally harming another inmate. All my hopes of having a conversation with anyone was dashed. I was now totally alone — and I did not know for how long this isolation would last.

For more than five months I lay curled up in my cell. No one spoke to me. Even the minister for the unit was not allowed to talk to me. In a way, I was dead. My mind, with no stimulation, floated in and out of consciousness. Time was cold and unending, with no watch or clock to show the passing hours.

I sought refuge inside my soul. I had only God to share these horrific moments with, and I felt he had let me down. His anger and his constant punishments left me without feeling or hope. I hated him. I was convinced God was uncaring at best, perhaps vindictive. This sense of him would carry on for many years after that.

I was in my cell, curled up on the bed. In Victoria, my nephew was receiving counselling. And his psychologist could find no evidence that he been abused or treated inappropriately. Looking back, I realize that shouldn't be surprising. While my sister never really believed I had shaken her child, she still would not have allowed me to be in a position to do the things I was accused of.

But a black, black picture had been painted of me. And so I was pushed away from the family — except from my dad — and was never really fully welcomed back by my older sister or my nephews.

The court, the penal system, the psychiatrist — surely they must have known I wasn't guilty of "sexual interference," that the charges were based on false statements I had made while in a psychotic state, a hoax. I was being punished for nothing more than being creative in my thinking and not knowing the consequences, given my distance from reality. Only about 10 years later did a psychiatrist tell me that I was innocent when I described my time at Colony Farm. He may have had access to files from that period, or he may have just made a conclusion based on my previous history with Borderline Personality Disorder and psychosis.

My world was a small, cold cell, without conversation or warmth. I came to mistrust people more and more. My physical safety was so compromised that I feared constantly for my life — even though I wished it would end.

Having no privacy was the biggest threat. I feared being abused by the male guards as they hovered around me in the washroom and the showers. They seemed overly interested in watching me doing my routine toileting. I had heard on the television many times when I was growing up how guards took advantage of inmates when they were most vulnerable, and I felt most vulnerable in their presence. I did not know what to expect or when to expect it. I think the only sanity-saving method I had to deal with this humiliation and potential threat was to return to my world of daydreams and blot out what was happening with me in the moment. My dreaming helped me bear the time with these guards and also my time in the cell. After a while, though, I could no longer daydream. The constant solitude paralyzed my thoughts and I existed in a constant state of numbness. All I could do was curl up in a ball and sleep — but most of the time not dream.

I "celebrated" my 40th birthday in prison. My dad and older sister came over from Victoria to spend an hour with me. I had known that my dad was coming but I wasn't expecting Joan. I knew my dad wanted to see how I was doing, because I had the opportunity only once to phone him from the prison. I think Joan, however, wanted to see what prisons looked like up close and personal. I was allowed out of my cell for the visit, but I was no mood to celebrate. I had asked the guards to let me wear my own clothes, instead of the prison uniform — for me, blue pajamas with a shirt that stayed unbuttoned, letting my breasts blatantly wave to all who were in contact with me, and bottoms that were too small and too tight. Laughing, the guards took me to a cupboard in the sleeping unit, opened it and told me I had to find something there to wear. Horrible polyester clothes, much, much too big, nothing that matched. After picking out an outfit and dressing, I was marched to the community room to greet my family. No matter how much they tried to lift my spirits, I was beyond even being able to talk with them. When they left for Victoria again after a short one-hour visit, I was taken out of the clothes and forced back to the cell.

I stayed there for three more weeks before being told I was to be released in a week.

I hadn't seen the outdoors for months, but I was given "privileges" to wander the grounds that last week before release. A CP Rail line ran through the farm, where some inmates worked. Once I had the right to walk outside, I contemplated jumping in front of the train. After one walk, I let the psychiatrist know that I planned to jump in front of the train.

"Not possible," he said. The train would stop before hitting me, as the engineer was schooled in the necessity to watch out for destructive inmates.

A week later, a social worker arrived to drive me to the bus station. I was free. I was also terrified, and feeling defeated and alone.

20 FREE, NOT FREE

Motel life, like apartment life and prison life, did not suit me. The darkness and the stillness ate at my soul. I was in a limbo that I could not crawl out of. I spent my days, my agoraphobic days, imprisoned inside my room. The highlight of these days, besides using and listening to mean, demanding voices in my head, was the walk to the hardware store to stock up on my escape juice.

I lived in this prison of a room without any activities or, for the most part, visitors. On a couple of occasions my dad and stepmom came to "check up on me." Satisfied that at least I had a roof over my head at that moment, they walked back out into the scary dark night.

When I was released from prison, I was subject to three years of supervision by a despicable probation officer who constantly threatened to send me back to jail because he was so sure I would "re-offend," when in fact I had never offended.

My probation scared me so much that the weekly bus trip across the city to the meet the probation officer threw me into a state of terror. He made it clear he hated me for my wrongdoings and that I was scum, and did not deserve any mercy from him.

I was receiving no real help or treatment while I was at the motel. I interacted occasionally with the Mental Health Centre, but with no real involvement. Case workers were a peripheral part of my live — around, but not playing an active role. I was on very little medication, as doctors feared that, given my suicidal thoughts, I might use it to end my life. But I was never hospitalized while I lived at the motel — mostly because, I believe, the system had not really recognized that I had returned to Victoria.

I wanted to die more than ever before, but I was usually too frightened to leave the motel room, especially in daylight, for fear of being snatched up by the police, so I couldn't go and buy the means to eliminate my self. I felt so deeply hurt that I was being treated by the universe so terribly. But what could I expect? I had "committed" a humongous crime.

There was almost no community support. I lived on welfare, less than $600 a month. The motel room ate up more than half that amount, and the other half — well, I tried to spend it on food, but the pain of abandonment and guilt always sent me to the hardware store instead of to the café around the corner.

At first the manager of the motel was not aware of what I was doing. But my room was connected to his suite with a door that did not quite meet the ground, and I thought he must smell the fumes. Even at night, when I used in the bathroom with the door closed, the odours could escape. After a few minutes of huffing I quit worrying about whether I was polluting his suite, yet my guilt consumed me when I was sober. One day, after three or four weeks, I told him I was using and addicted to solvent — toluene to be exact.

He was appalled. He swore at me, screamed that his wife had lupus and I was compromising her health. I'd never heard of lupus and just ignored his yelling.

He told me I had six hours to get out.

Stoned, frightened and with absolutely nowhere to go, I phoned my sisters, my dad, friends — mostly from church — seeking asylum and refuge. No one would take me in. Finally, though I do not know why, I phoned the doctor I had at the time. With only an hour left on my eviction clock, she answered the phone. I told her I was about to be homeless; she hesitated and agreed to take me in. Thirty minutes later she pulled up at the motel, alone in an SUV to collect me and my bits and pieces of luggage. She was younger than I was, a single parent with three children — two girls (one about eight or nine and the other in her mid-teens) and one boy (about twelve). She was a general practitioner with a specialty in obstetrics. She had a fanatical laugh and I was amazed at how much energy she had. Her love for her children was overwhelming to me and I envied this.

Yet, despite all her kindness, I hated the ride to her place because I felt, just as I had many times before, that I was being rescued again. I had come to know that these "rescue" situations never turned out well — and I was always the one who produced the unhappy ending.

My doctor lived in Oak Bay, the snazzy part of town. I felt like a country bumpkin moving to New York City when I arrived that afternoon at her huge three-storey house with its tidy wood siding. Her medical office was in the basement at the back. I had been there many times before. She had taken me under her wing early on as my physician, offering empathy for my mental health and physical problems. Yet at the moment I arrived at her home to live, I felt I was a foreigner in an uncharted country.

I shared a room with one of my doctor's friends — a half-wall dividing us in the dark basement. This friend was gone most of the day, babysitting somewhere. Once again, I was lonely and isolated. I was supposed to be doing laundry and other bits of housework in return for room and board. But I rarely ate — no meals were offered, and I couldn't make myself venture into the kitchen to cook as I was depressed and paralyzed with fear of being seen. I wanted her and her family to pretend I wasn't there when they were home, so I remained quietly sitting in my "room" with nothing to do but live with my thoughts. When they were not home, I still stayed mostly in my room ,but did venture out to do my chores.

Neither the doctor nor her children believed in tidiness. Every day I was horrified at the mess they left after they went to school and work.

At first I felt obliged to clean up, but I grew more and more despondent at the impossibility of keeping order in their home, alone all day, with nothing to eat.

I wasn't using. But I was white-knuckling it — avoiding huffing through sheer effort, still desperate to use.

My doctor's medical office was opposite my basement room. In the evenings I started sneaking in, foraging for drugs and stealing samples I discovered in an office cupboard. My doctor made a few comments that made me realize that she suspected, but I didn't care and didn't stop. My goal was to accumulate enough pills to be able to kill myself, not to get high. And by the time I eventually left her house for a new place, I had a plastic bag full of the stolen pills.

Christmas came. The doctor's family decorated the living room, but

I was not invited to join in the festivities. I had no contact with either friends or my family. I felt I had been, once again, abandoned because everyone knew I at least had a roof over my head — for the moment, anyway. My dad never came around nor phoned, nor did my sisters. My belief was they were happy to have a holiday from me.

I was lonely, sad and angry. However, on Christmas Eve, the doctor and her children took me to the Mormon Church, where they were members, for the Christmas Eve service. I was fascinated by the warmth of their greeting of me, a non-Mormon, though I could not help but notice that there were parts of this church I was not allowed to enter. I did not understand their ceremony, yet I enjoyed it — it was so different and so refreshing a view of the Christmas story, and I was swept away by it.

After Christmas they all went back to school and work, and I was left to clean up the Christmas debris and put away the ornaments and tree. The windows had fake snow sprayed all over them and the doctor gave me a can of solvent and told me to clean them. I hated the idea — until I found that the snow remover was full of toluene.

Joyously, I began sniffing, my brief period of sobriety abandoned. My weakness disgusted me, yet I could not stop. In the evenings, when they frequently all went out, I would take the solvent tin hidden under my pillow and, often sitting out on their balcony with the sliding doors shut, I began inhaling, constantly listening for sounds of their return — slamming car doors, footsteps and voices. I thought they did not know what I was doing, but now I am sure it must have been obvious, although no one said anything to me during my stay there.

About a month later, long after I had drained the solvent tin and been dry for about a week, I could no longer resist going to the hardware store on Oak Bay's small main street to buy thinner. With tin in hand that morning, I looked for a place where I could hide away and use. It was warmish, with a hint of spring, and I found a rock outcrop below the sidewalk near the Oak Bay Marina where I climbed down and huddled close to the salt water, trying to avoid detection. I do not know how long I was there, but by the time I belatedly noticed the tide was coming in I was almost too stoned to climb back up the rocks. Scared, panicky and holding onto the solvent tin with a strong grasp, I scrambled up the rocky slope on my knees. Once back on the sidewalk I stumbled home.

I learned early in my habit that once I started sniffing, I could not stop. There was still thinner left in the tin, so when I got back home I sat in a chair that was stuffed into my dark semi-room, and continued where I had left off at the marina. My roommate came home for a short time but seemed awfully eager to leave again. I didn't care. We never talked to each other; we co-existed. Left alone in the basement once again, I continued my trek into oblivion.

My behaviour was causing a huge rift between my doctor, her family and me. I was given the coldest of shoulders and finally reached out to a social worker at the local mental health centre I attended sporadically. I told him about my living arrangements and he listened with great compassion and said he would find a new place for me to live — something more suitable than anything I had in the past.

Within a few weeks I was being driven by the mental health worker and my new case manager to Esquimalt to visit McAndrew Lodge, an independent psychiatric boarding home. They introduced me to the manager and staff, showed me around, and we left.

About a week later the workers picked me up from the doctor's home once again and delivered me to the lodge, where I stayed for more than 18 months, never using, but often making suicidal gestures by scratching up my arms. But during that period, for the first time ever, I felt that I could belong somewhere, even though I was standoffish because I was afraid of the people living in the lodge.

Life in the boarding home was challenging, and once again I felt lonely. In the first couple of months I ended up in the hospital at least three times because I could not get enough sleep. I shared a small, small room with two other very ill women. The roommate who slept closest to my bed, about an arm's length away, talked non-stop to herself all night. I could not sleep with this going on and often would get so angry that I would throw my pillow at her and yell at her to shut up. The other roommate would constantly jump out of bed and open the door to the room, letting in all the light from the hall. As I was such a light sleeper and suffered terribly from insomnia, being kept awake pushed me into manic spaces. Instinctively I tried to work off the mania by doing the gardening at the home, working from dawn to dusk, day after day. Summer and warmer days was coming, but I couldn't stand being indoors with all the "loonies." I had no reason to explore the neighbourhood and was too afraid to walk anywhere anyway, knowing I had to remain sober. Gardening became my new addiction as I hauled out weeds and plants, practically devastating the front gardens. In the end, I was taken to the hospital to settle down. Medicated more and more, I would return back to the lodge depressed and still unable to fit in.

It took three visits to the hospital before the doctors recommended to the staff that I get my own room, and I did.

I found life in the boarding home intensely difficult. Often I felt like I was being constantly watched. On my first day, while doing the required bath, the manager walked into the bathroom with a pearl necklace in her hand to "give to me." I realized instantly that personal privacy was not respected in this new place either. After that, the manager was always calling me into her office for one thing or other and I, not knowing her real aim, became cautious of her attentions and avoided her whenever I could.

However, it seemed God had a plan for me — a wonderful plan. Just like new life in a garden in spring, new life was beginning to take hold of me. I had been toying with the idea of returning to a small, wooden heritage church down the road from McAndrew Lodge — St. Paul's on Esquimalt Road. Finally, I took the first steps to returning to the Anglican Church.

21 REACHING OUT

My loneliness in the lodge shaped my life. I felt I was above the other tenants intellectually and emotionally. I was craving attention and validation.

As I was generally self-sufficient, the rules and daily schedule meant little to me. We were to be up by seven o'clock, dressed and ready for the day by eight, then breakkie. Lunch at noon and dinner at five. There was a lot of free time that most of the residents spent watching TV. Some of the residents would walk around the neighbourhood and some would even venture into town with the help of a $45 annual bus pass.

Most of the other people at the Lodge seemed to need immeasurable assistance, especially the men who lined up in the hallway every morning to be shaved and have their hair combed and trimmed by the staff. I could see no point in this — the lodge was simply mollycoddling them out of taking responsibility for themselves. Most of the residents were extremely ill, and over-medicating was the practice of the day, making it almost impossible for them to do any form of self-care without direction or intervention. But while I objected, I too longed for such focused attention.

In many ways I felt trapped, as I was afraid to venture out on my own to explore the world around the lodge. So I channeled my energy into being an advocate for the residents and others in the same situation, writing innumerable letters to the government requesting higher disability assistance rates and other improvements that would have made a great difference in our lives.

Most of us were living on provincial government disability assistance. After the lodge was paid for our room and board, we were left with about $80 a month for all other expenses. It was a hardship living on a pittance of about $2.70 a day for clothes, personal items, any transportation. I never had enough to buy books and magazines, to buy postage stamps for the occasional letter I wrote, or even for treats from the local shopping plaza on Esquimalt Road near our place. For sure I never had any money to go on a holiday, so I was trapped, more or less, at the lodge, without any hope of going anywhere to get away from it all.

At least at the beginning, I held myself captive in my long, dark room with my typewriter and a television set my father had brought me. I was able to bring some of my own possessions into my room — particularly books and a sewing machine, which I used to make quilts from donated material and batting. Eventually I started collecting belongings like dishes, a vacuum cleaner, linens and towels, and put them under my bed for the moment I would get my own apartment. I was on the waiting list for a supported independent living program through Capital Mental Health, which would allow me to live "on my own" with workers' support. My belongings, ones I could use at the lodge and the others for my future semi-independent living, helped me feel less disconnected from my past life.

Yet this wasn't enough to satisfy my cravings for companionship and intellectual conversation. I would act out to gain attention, often by cutting myself, but instead of attention I was given large doses of chlorpromazine which made me sleep for days on end, being woken to take bathroom breaks and not much else. I often longed for the escape of those drugged days to reduce the ennui of life in the lodge. But when I eventually woke up, I was left disoriented and more isolated.

I was resourceful though. I watched the lodge owner come and go, fixing things that were out of place, stopping to talk to residents. Somehow I connected with her. I knew she was a lesbian and, although I was hesitant to reveal my orientation, I knew she knew I was one too. We had long, long chats about everything imaginable every time she came to the lodge. The intellectual and emotional stimulation was just what I needed, but it didn't last.

The on-site manager, either out of jealousy or spite, stopped these interactions from taking place after a few months. Most of the time, she would call me into her office (and I would go shaking) and tell me to stay away from the manager. She kept on telling me that I had to stop and that my long conversations with the owner prevented her from getting the necessary repairs done. I would stop for a few days, hoping to let the wind of authority blow itself out or that the manager would somehow forget that she warned me. During those few days I would aimlessly wander around the lodge or lay motionless on my bed, lost without anything to do. Once again, I felt stranded and betrayed by the manager's demands. I was angry and bereft.

I was desperate for positive human contact, and started to help out in the kitchen. I had a crush on the cook and I wanted so much to be around her. I would work all day, peeling veggies, doing dishes — anything that I could do. I had a wonderful time and felt useful and acknowledged. Again, this came to an end when the on-site manager forced me to leave the kitchen. In the end, she assigned me to wash down the kitchen every evening after the last dish was taken from our powerful dishwasher. I hated this chore. Lonely and disgusted in my new role, I would hurry through. I could not understand why I had to do this every evening. For some reason, eventually, I was given freedom from this task.

The whole time I was at the lodge, I never resorted to using solvent. I missed it, and would fantasize for hours and hours about obtaining it and hiding somewhere along the Songhees waterfront walkway near "home." Perhaps I never had the courage to play the scene out in reality. Perhaps, knowing my stay at the lodge was always in the balance, I did try to stick to activities and behaviours that would ensure I wasn't kicked out.

I did attend church, sporadically at first. I had returned to the cathedral downtown. However, I was not satisfied and so, after learning there was a small, heritage Anglican church, St. Paul's (now St. Peter's and St. Paul's) just a few blocks down the road from the house, I wrote to the minister to gain permission to attend.

This odd little man — my first impression of him — permitted me to come and talk with him at the church one day. He too found me odd, in that I had requested a visit to clinch permission to attend — and attend I did.

Reverend Michael Piddington became a lifelong friend until he passed away in September 2016. He and his wife Patricia, took me under their wings and adopted me into their family and life. For really the first time in my entire life, I felt important; I felt loved; and I felt accepted for who I really was. They offered unconditional and ever flowing love.

The focus of my life began to change. Shy and uncomfortable as I was, I attended St. Paul's regularly. The short walk to church every Sunday morning invigorated me and I felt free.

I first met Patricia one Sunday at the coffee hour after the church service. She approached me and began chatting. Not knowing who she was, I followed her around the hall next to the church as she poured me a cup of tea and sat me down. She was so interested in me. Before long I realized she was the minister's wife, and I was honoured and humbled by her presence. We became instant friends, just as her husband had. Often Pat would meet me for coffee at the corner coffee shop in the plaza near the lodge and she would chat in her animated manner.

I remember how strange her attention felt and, naturally, my fear that it would end, as always such relationships did. But it didn't. At first I couldn't understand, as she would talk about her day-to-day life and not focus on me. All my life, the focus was on me anytime I interacted with another person. I couldn't explain this to her.

However, I came to realize that this woman was sharing her life with me. She was a home care worker and a mother of four — two of her children were adopted — and so interested in the world around. Pat was medium height, simply dressed, slightly chubby, with a huge, tender smile. She had no frills in dress or speech that would distract anyone from her genuine caring.

And she was an artist. Though I wasn't into art much at the time, when she showed me her studio, nestled in the basement of her home, it sparked an interest in me that would one day ignite. She did woodcut prints, and I was so impressed by the detail she could obtain with the chisels. I remembered a night school woodcarving course I had taken while still living at home. I was not successful and tossed both the tools and the memories aside once the course was completed — I deemed the process too difficult to ever carve something recognizable. But Pat helped me appreciate the wood, the meditative carving and the prints produced in the end. She often branched out by doing upholstering and sewing, and was skilled at both.

Pat kept in touch with me, and I continued to attend the church, after my stay in the lodge ended. I helped her in many ways — once I did the dishes for one of her New Year's open houses and she remained at my side somehow, supportive and encouraging, while at the same time hostessing her party. Another day I spent out in her garden with a trowel transplanting some plants into her well-tended, and much enjoyed, flower garden. I began to love her deeply. She walked with me through the darkness and the manic highs of my life, never criticizing or giving advice, just taking me as I was. This is where the hope for my life started to develop.

Mike and Pat were building a home on the south side of Shawnigan Lake, about 45 kilometres from Victoria. Pat would bundle me into the car and we would drive up regularly to check on the construction. I recall days when it was so, so cold outside. She plunged enthusiastically into supervising the design of her new home and, with just as much excitement, purchased all the hardware, flooring, roofing and whatever else the home needed.

I could not understand why someone would be so interested in building a house. My take on this was that no one stayed in their homes more than a few months — I certainly didn't — so why all the fuss? Somehow I never fully appreciated her dream home or her simple, humble life. I wished I had been more attentive to her excitement and vision. I still was so focused on myself, lapping up the attention.

Then Pat was diagnosed with colon cancer. I ended up in the psych unit at the hospital shortly after learning of her illness, so overwrought that head banging became a daily activity.

Once I was released after about three months in hospital, I lovingly took the train to Shawnigan Lake for visits with Pat, who was living out the last of her days in the house she had poured her heart and soul into.

At first she was able to meet the train with Michael, but soon the trip around the lake became too difficult for her. She spent her days bedridden, peering out the window at the lake.

I was so fearful of her death. I felt like the only hope in my life was being torn from me. I cried and cried, inconsolable, as her life was closing. My life had returned to emptiness.

Pat died in May 1997. I was 47. She was the first person ever that stayed in any of my apartments, willingly sleeping on the hard floor behind my living room couch for a week. I had had breast reduction surgery early on in our friendship and she offered to stay with me to make sure I was OK. Her warmth, dedication and willingness to be at my side moved me. No one had ever done this before.

She even attended my graduation from business school in the mid 1990s, along with my father, and helped me find my first job in many years. I was living in my semi-independent apartment on Lampson Street, and decided to return to business school so that I could, eventually, get a job and make some extra money to allow me to have a few frills in my life — going out for tea or buying new clothes.

Pat had walked a new, unfamiliar path with me. She had empowered me. I was to take some of this love and caring with me into a new adventure.

At her funeral in Cobble Hill I sobbed uncontrollably through the entire service, and was glad my sister Anne and her partner Betty had come with me. It was months, even years, before I could stop myself fom crying any time I thought about Pat. Eventually I had to wipe her from my mind and refuse to think of her in order to get on with my life. Not until my mid-60s, as I began writing this book, would I allow myself to remember her with the sorrow and sweetness she brought to my life. Painful as my memories are now, I am glad I have let Pat back into my consciousness. I feel more whole now, emotionally, as a result of this.

Michael never let me wander away from his family — either emotionally or physically. He knew the depth of my sorrow and the journey Pat and I had shared. Michael honoured what Pat had shared with me. Even when I was so, so mentally sick and, once again, addicted, he never abandoned me — never.

This very painful chapter of my life helped me take awkward new steps into being aware and caring for others, even if it was fleeting. I had a new awareness about myself. And yes, I knew I was loved.

22 HOSPITAL AND A NEW HOME

As my friendship with Pat and Michael grew, my life in the lodge shrank. My days were lonely and frightening and, ultimately, disastrous. I so much wanted to get away from the lodge because the behaviour of some staff reminded me of the ways my mother had directed her anger at me as I was growing up. They would give me the cold shoulder and refuse to speak to me. I was dumbfounded, but muddled through as I dealt with their apparent angry behaviour.

More and more I wanted just to move away — move away from the discomfort and the confusion. I still had my sights on the semi-independent living program, however it was seemingly so far away in the future. But I never even dreamed that I would be sent away from the lodge.

Things came to a head after a trip with a group of residents to a lodge on Sproat Lake. I so enjoyed myself, opting to be one of the main cooks for the herd. I was elated by my holiday, but the day I returned home I experienced a great coldness from the nurse and was not greeted by her. I sensed that I had done something incredibly wrong; however to this day I do not know what had stuck in her craw. I was deflated by the nurse's obvious dislike of me.

I was devastated. I hurried to my room and downed a whole bottle of Tylenol that I had hidden in my belongings. Then I took a utility knife and slashed open my side. When the staff discovered me, I bolted out the front door of the boarding home and fled down the street, crying my heart out as a staff person pursued me. In the end, not knowing where I was headed, puffed out, I was still not happy when the person caught up to me — with a police car following him. Whisked away to the hospital emergency department, I was then held captive in the psych unit once again, this time never to return to the lodge. My dad was forced to come and pick up all my belongings, which were strewn over the front lawn.

I had been in the hospital for about a month when the social worker I had at McAndrew Lodge came to visit me. She told me that she had found a new boarding home for me.

That wasn't what I wanted to hear. For over a year, since the beginning of 1990, I had been waiting for a supported independent living program to begin. The program was a joint project between the Greater Victoria Hospital Society and Capital Mental Health. It offered freedom — the chance to live on my own for the first time in years, while having support from the Capital Mental Health independent living team to help me cope so I wouldn't be hospitalized so often. In my last three or four months at McAndrew, I had been hounding the doctors and support workers to get me into this program, constantly begging the workers who were planning it to get the program started.

But it still wasn't ready to begin, so I ended up in another boarding home that my social worker had found. To my relief, this boarding home was a far sight better than McAndrew and I felt, finally, I had hit the jackpot.

Greenridge, considered the best boarding home in the mental health system, was nestled on a steep hill along the perimeter of the Swan Lake Nature Sanctuary in Saanich. I found life more carefree and relaxing than at McAndrew Lodge. The residents, somewhere around eight to ten of them, were more at my intellectual level as well as much more emotionally compatible. The residents of McAndrew never seemed to have a grasp of the basics of looking after themselves, but at Greenwood everyone knew how to toilet themselves, how to fill spare time, how to converse with one another. We were all responsible for doing the chores around the place, taking turns vacuuming and cooking, particularly. We were responsible for keeping our rooms tidy and making and keeping appointments, with most of us attending them on our own. We had privileges and were treated as adults, not like children as at McAndrew. There was nothing punitive about Greenridge. I was accepted there with open arms.

We were a motley crew of mixed genders, but we got along reasonably well, and the staff were caring, supportive and encouraging. During my time at Greenridge I attended the day hospital at the Eric Martin Pavilion next door to the Mental Heath Centre I was enrolled in a program to learn life skills to help me live more successfully on my own — how to cook, budget my money, keep an apartment clean and do laundry, as well as how to plan spare time. Also, there were courses on dealing with anger and depression. I experienced a lot of both — even more so as I stayed sober.

I hated some of the program, especially the part on trying to plan my spare time. For the most part I was not interested in community activities, mainly because of my agoraphobia. So I sucked up to the staff and did everything I could to receive accolades from them. I was a model "student."

After three months at Greenridge, I knew I was ready to move on to the supported independent living program. I kept pressing the people creating and managing the program to accept me. And finally, my hounding worked. I was admitted as the first resident in the program in January 1992.

It seemed an easy transition. I was ready, more confident in my skills and my determination to make this move to semi-independent living successful.

The day of my move, my sister and dad came to Greenridge and piled my small nest of belongings into the back of a U-Haul — mostly clothes, a record player and records, and some small pieces of furniture. I was worried on moving day because it had snowed the night before and the roads were slippery. But my sister Anne, a trouper, manoeuvred the truck through downtown Victoria and across the Johnson Street bridge to Esquimalt and my new apartment, just around the corner from McAndrew Lodge. My dad had been shopping at The Brick and bought me a bed, so it was the first item pushed through the door of my apartment. The moving took less than a half-hour, and once my furniture — a few bits that had been stored at my dad's place, a dresser, TV, clothes and odds and ends — were unloaded, my family went off.

Waiting with me was Pat Piddington, who had rags and buckets in hand to help me wash down the apartment. Pat, a home care worker, started with the cupboard under the kitchen sink, laughingly telling me that was often the one place that NEVER got cleaned by the departing tenants — and she was right. We found a stash of empty pop and beer bottles and Pat returned them to the store for refunds; days later the former tenants were knocking on my door, adamantly wanting them back — or at least the money. Pat, standing next to me, boldly told them that it was a clear case of "finders keepers" and sent them on their way. They were so very angry that I feared retribution at some later date, but they never came back.

By the second day I was officially moved in. Pictures on the wall — well, one picture I had bought on Boxing Day at Kmart before moving — and towels in the bathroom, bathtub sparkling, floors shining and curtains on the windows glowing. My apartment felt like a small, cozy, feather-padded nest.

The best part was that I finally was alone. It seemed a little celebration was needed, so when Pat had gone for the day I walked up the hill to Esquimalt Road and the Canadian Tire at Head Street. I bought a tin of lacquer thinner. Feeling creepy as I sniffed away the rest of the day, I became fearful of being evicted, even though the landlord knew nothing of my habit. Sometime during my time with the solvent I must have phoned Greenridge. A staff member, worried by my call and the state I was in, came to get me and whisked me back to the boarding home to stay an extra few nights.

I stayed at Greenridge for several days, venturing to my apartment in the daytime and getting acquainted with the neighbourhood. After about a week of this, I was permitted to move into my new home.

For about three years — from 1992 until 1996— I remained sober. At first I was white-knuckling it, struggling to make it through each day without using and feeling so very self-conscious about conversing with other people. I felt awkward in body and mind and knew I just wasn't community savvy after spending most of my adult life in hospital or stoned. Though the supported independent living program staff kept in close touch during this time, taking me to buy groceries and run errands and, sometimes, just for a ride around the city, I was aware that I was still afraid to venture out alone much. So I remained alone in my apartment much of the time, left to the thoughts of guilt and unworthiness that were still a huge part of my life. Yet my life began to unfold, this time taking a different route than I had ever taken before. I had rarely been clean and sober while living on my own, so I was challenged daily, often seemingly beyond my capacity to manage.

Pat was always there for me, and helped me leap hurdles that I never dreamed I could. Life became good, and even today I marvel at this adventure in reasonably successful independent living — at least at first it was successful.

This new chapter in my life had begun.

23 LIFE ON MY OWN

For the first few years of living on my own I struggled with everyday life sober. My confidence was tested and my agoraphobia magnified, but I managed to keep house, buy groceries and survive in my new surroundings. All my life I struggled with agoraphobia — fear of being outside. Often this was the deciding factor in my inability to work. I just could not get out of the apartment. The only place I knew I could get to, with a lot of trepidation, was the hardware store.

Sober, I found my agoraphobia more crippling than ever. Not only did I not have the hardware store as a consistent destination, I had great anxiety about having to go to the grocery store or the bank, which were just around the corner from me at the Esquimalt plaza. I stayed home and cowered most of the time. This eventually caused a rift between me and my sisters, as I could never seem to grab a bus and go to their places or even to their planed events. If it wasn't for the independent living program taking me out weekly, I am pretty sure I would never have been able to get groceries or cash my disability cheques.

I received about $770 in disability assistance, but more than three-quarters of that went to pay my rent. Even with a rent subsidy of about $125 a month from Capital Mental Health, it was a challenge to budget and survive now that I was on my own. I had a very limited income after paying rent, less than $300 a month, to cover food, clothes, transportation — everything. I survived those first few years on a little money, but it was hard. And to make it harder, I just could not get the hang of this budgeting stuff. I had no idea about cheque writing, for example, and would find myself in great debt at the beginning of each month when the bank statements and NSF cheques started to arrive in my mailbox.

I enrolled in Laurel Enterprises, a Capital Mental Health program aimed at preparing people for work or volunteer opportunities, and was able to earn a few dollars in training pay every month. This program frightened me, though I was encouraged to attend by my case manager. I sensed that I just wasn't cut out for the work force. Computers were now a big part of working life, and I did not enjoy messing around with them one iota. Basically I was attending the program for the $100 a month offered to participants. The one part I absolutely loved was woodworking. Working with tools — large and small — gave me a sense of satisfaction and mastery. I could have spent hours and hours in the workshop, but our days were broken up into periods and we would go from one activity to another. And, of course, one of the other activities was computers! I cringed every time I knew my next period was typing and learning computer skills.

I came to rely on this money, so when my stint at Laurel Enterprises ended after two years I moved into a volunteer position at the Esquimalt Neighbourhood House. Though the position was voluntary, it qualified me for a few dollars a month as part of social services ministry work program.

My stability was up and down during these first few years on my own. Relying on my manic stages to propel me from the house, I would report to the neighbourhood house office, doing photocopying, filing, typing and answering the phone. I grew comfortable in this position and enjoyed, somewhat, the interactions with the public and the staff. My shyness, though still powerful, was not crippling me. In the end I thrived there and felt successful. The routine suited me and the contact was sufficient to endorse my worthiness.

Throughout my adult life I volunteered a lot when I was not working, testing my worth and seeking to fulfill my need for validation and approval. I was uncomfortable emotionally in most of these situations, relying on my solvent habit to get me through. However, at Esquimalt Neighbourhood House, I flourished while sober.

By 1994, I felt strong enough to enrol in CompuCollege to brush up my secretarial skills. The course was tough for me, especially the interactions with the other students. I felt inept and awkward as my school mates shared laughter and stories. I had no idea how to have a conversation or join in a group — and, for the most part, I still can't do this. I tended to keep to myself and would rush home after the day at school and lock myself in my apartment.

The supported independent living program kept me afloat. There were weekly visits from the staff, taking me for groceries or on errands or outings. I came to rely on their presence as my anchor when I set out on frightening adventures in the new outside world. The workers marvelled at my "more or less" independence — not only from the boarding homes, but from my drug. I relished their attention. I needed their support more than ever when I went back to school, and I got it. As frightened as I was about my studies, I grew into the comfortable school schedule for almost nine months — then once again, this routine ended.

On one of my visits to Capital Mental Health on Skinner Street, where Laurel Enterprises was located, I ran into Gail Simpson, the executive director. She asked me if I would like to sit on the board of Canadian Mental Health and, with great fear, I said "Yes." As a board member, I took on the role of representing Victoria and southern Vancouver Island at meetings of the CMHA's B.C. division. For three years I travelled to Vancouver every few months for the board meetings. I took copious notes so that I could go back to my board in Victoria with a detailed update of what happened in the meetings. However, once again my shyness, emotional instability and outright fear prevented me from interacting with the others. Though this was a mental health organization, no one really took notice of me, and I felt so terribly lonely at these meetings, unable to speak up at roundtable discussions and horrified when I was forced to give my opinion.

Travelling to the meetings was also challenging. My agoraphobia was pushed to its limit as I travelled alone, by Greyhound bus and ferry, to the YWCA in downtown Vancouver for the meetings. They were often over two or three days. In the evening, when everyone else was out having fun, I was locked in my hotel room, panicking and isolated.

There was never any fun for me. I would venture out to the McDonald's around the corner from the YWCA for meals and scurry home again. I felt like a foreigner and a prisoner at the same time.

I am not sure to this day how I kept on going back to the meetings. The whole thing was torture. Yet I kept going; my pride needed to be fed. My reports to the local CMHA branch, though very long indeed, brought me the acknowledgement I so needed— perhaps that was enough to keep me participating in the B.C. board meetings.

A few years later, I became president of our local branch and I ran the meetings with an iron fist, with no dawdling in discussions. I pushed through conversations and motions quickly — because I just wanted to go home and be alone.

Working with the CMHA board was challenging. I would easily get bored by the long, long conversations of some of the members — conversations that seemed circular in content, the same points getting repeated over and over again. I never really contributed much verbally and felt dumb and small, yet I wanted to do something to give back to my world and the programs trying to support my independence.

But, oddly, I discovered that while individual conversations and small groups were torture, speaking to groups seemed so much easier. I did a few television interviews about the program, and found I was relaxed and able to speak easily. The same was true for speeches to groups. One CMHA conference trip took me to Quebec City to report on the supported independent living program — both how I got involved in getting it off the ground and how the program assisted my independence. My speech was well received and I realized that I was comfortable speaking to a sea of unfamiliar faces. My sentences and thoughts flowed. I seemed to flourish in this role, which was a great boost to my ego.

Travel to these meetings was a different story. I had only been on an airplane once before, in handcuffs as I was taken from prison in the Lower Mainland to Victoria. Travelling alone across the country scared me so much I had flatulence the whole trip. My seat partner stopped talking to me within a few minutes after take-off. When I returned home from Quebec City I vowed never to travel alone or fly again, and crawled back into my apartment, shut the doors and window, and lay on my couch for days, refusing to move or even to feed myself.

But while every journey was horrendous, I endured them and ultimately felt some sense of freedom by doing so. I did overcome my fear and go to conferences again, once in Toronto and then in Hamilton. Still socially inept, I did enjoy getting away from Victoria and seeing a little of Canada. I would spend my spare time in the evenings in my hotel room, again not interacting in the fun events of the conference. I believe now that I stuck to the CMHA board for the travelling experiences. The conferences seemed worth the stress of the board work and taxing of my fearful soul. So, for about four years, I continued to sit on the board.

My studies continued during this time. A few times I was named student of the week at the college. What was supposed to be an honour was an embarrassment to me. My photo was plastered on the hallway wall, open to inspection by the students. I wanted so much to remain invisible that even the recognition did not nurture me. In the end, I graduated with first class honours and I was proud to have endured this and come out on top — or so I thought.

The graduation ceremony was held at the Victoria Conference Centre, attached to the posh Empress Hotel. I had nothing to wear. So I asked Capital Mental Health for a grant to buy a skirt and blouse for the occasion. Skirts were not my thing in those days; I wore slacks and jeans most of the time. When I put my skirt on I became aware that my body had become heavy and, in my thoughts, very ugly indeed.

Pat Piddington, bless her soul, lent me a pair of her shoes — much too big for me, so I stuffed them with cardboard so they almost fit. I clumped around the conference centre before the ceremony; I clumped up to the stage to receive my certificate; I clumped home. Both Pat and my dad attended as moral support, and met each other for the first time. In the end, the evening brought me satisfaction and relief. I had endured the course.

Luck shined on me. I did not really have to look for work after finishing the course. A job as an assistant in a denture clinic more or less fell into my lap the week before I was to leave the college. A woman from my church was set to fill this position, but at the last minute she had to back out. She mentioned to the denturist that I had just graduated and asked if he would interview me. Interview me he did. He had phoned me to come in the Friday before my course ended and, after a short conversation, he asked me to return the following Monday to start — three afternoons a week from 1 to 5 p.m. as the receptionist/secretary and the janitor. Neither of us were keen about me taking the position, I suspect. But I got the job. I finished at the college on a Friday and started work on the Monday. My trepidation grew once again.

My work involved assisting in the clinic and answering calls. But I was scared of both the public and the telephone, so afraid of saying the wrong things to people that I spoke softly so that my boss wouldn't hear me. Phoning people to confirm their appointments was torture, and I pleaded with God to ensure they wouldn't answer so I could just leave a message. That was not as hard.

However, the thorn in my side was the bookkeeping — I could never balance the books. I was to enter all the money that was brought in by the clinic daily, tallying up the money. Each time I tallied I got a different number and, after hours of slaving over the figures, I would just pick one and write it down. I never spoke with anyone about the way I was doing the books with the hope that somehow, magically, the problem would sort itself out. I simply did not know what I was doing. I was so frightened about being found out that I had nightmares every night. My terror gripped me in every waking hour. If my inability was discovered, I thought, it would be the worst humiliation ever.

I eventually retreated to my bed on my days off. I didn't want to talk to anyone or go out; I didn't know how to have a life between shifts. I lasted 18 months in this job.. By then I was ill, mentally and with stomach problems, and I quit.

I was lucky enough to get back onto full disability assistance and just hid away in my apartment, basically only going out for board meetings. But once again, I did not have enough money to live on. So I took the first steps toward conjuring up a way to earn a few bucks, and my idea for a recreational and visiting program started to take form.

I was still sober and supported independent living was still in the picture.

24 I CREATE A PROGRAM

In spite of my extreme shyness, I had begun to take on other activities as a mental health advocate. I was a guest speaker at the University of Victoria's introduction to social work program several times. My goal was to give the students some insights about what mental illness, and social work, meant to me. I spoke about my interactions with the social services ministry and the social workers in the psychiatric hospitals, as well as my experiences with mental illness.

I was an expert, having spent so much of my life in the hospital. When I was in my 20s, the hospital filled my need for routine and for social fun. Even though I did not talk much, I loved the various events. Social workers, both in the hospital and in the ministry system, were most often delighted to help me get in and out of various community programs. The nurses and social workers really did provide me with a sense of purpose and, even though I was generally isolated out in the community, I did achieve an element of "success."

In the beginning, the social workers and nurses were a lifeline, giving me a reason to get out and about. But as time went along I became afraid of them, mostly because I did not want to be "out and about," I wanted to be left alone in my apartment. My fears of being in the outside world were intensifying. I lived under the belief that no one knew about my addiction, so when I had to make an appointment with a worker I would fight for days to stay sober so I wouldn't be found out. I felt that I was "ripping off" the system and they might think I was too lazy to work. As time went on, I began to feel ashamed at my inability to function in the workplace and my lack of sobriety, and any contact with workers made me feel so much a failure. In the end, social workers and nurses took on the role of demons in my mind and I tried, at all costs — using and withdrawing into myself—to avoid them.

I look back now and realize the workers knew I couldn't function in the workplace and had an overwhelming addiction.

After several talks with the university social work students, I was asked to make a tape of my speech for the social work department's distance learning program. One day, I was whisked up to the university by my friends and supporters Rosalie Goldstein and Diane de Champlain, who were professors in the social work program. I sat for more than two hours in a small, stuffy room on campus, with a technical student to operate the recording equipment. The taping went well and, exhausted by the procedure, I returned home. This tape was used for years and years.

To my surprise, I was in my glory speaking to the students, and my confidence had been boosted, at least somewhat.

After a few more visits to speak to the social work students, I moved on. I was still active in the Canadian Mental Health Association's Victoria branch and began to think of my next move. Realizing I could make a difference in the understanding of mental illness and health, in 1996 I approached CMHA executive director Gail Simpson to ask for funding for a program I had begun to develop to improve the lives of people in group homes. The CMHA board voted to provide $200 a month to set up and run the recreational and visiting program.

After months of struggling with WordPerfect on my home computer to prepare brochures, and photocopying endless drafts of program ideas on the Capital Mental Health photocopying machine, I was ready to begin searching for volunteers.

Initially I ran the program on my own. It was new and my concept was different, based on a discussion I had with the director of Big Brothers and Big Sisters Victoria. That organization paired adult volunteers with children in need of support or mentorship. I wanted to create a buddy system for residents of group homes.

When I lived in McAndrew Lodge, I came to see boarding homes were warehouses for mentally ill people who had very little contact with the outside world. I saw that many of my fellow residents had few visitors — some had none — and little opportunity to leave the lodge.

Pat's visits and her role in showing me the world, often taking me out of my dark, dingy room at the lodge for outings, led me to think of creating this program.

Now that I was in the supported independent living program, I felt I could open up some doors for group home clients across the region. One of the members of the CMHA board, Barbara Bawlf, became a supporter of the program. My agoraphobia was in full bloom, yet I needed to visit all the group homes in Victoria to share the program proposal and vision statement and talk with clients and staff to learn if my program would be useful for them. Barbara took the initiative and set up appointments with the homes. She was there to help me — very frightened — onto buses that took me into many uncharted areas of town. I was devastated and scared every single time, often thinking I could not carry out my mission. With Barb's support, we accomplished these visits.

I created brochures about the program, incorporating the information from the visits to the group homes, and began advertising for volunteers. I placed ads in the daily newspaper and community newspapers and put notices on bulletin boards in churches, rec centres and at the university bulletin boards — any place I could think of.

I started out with a small group which included a couple of university students, a newspaper reporter for the Victoria News, a Christian Wiccan and a couple of mental health clients. I was consumed by the various needs of my program and at one point held a make-do training program for my small group of helpers in my tiny apartment on Lampson Street. Even Gail Simpson came.

Finally, we were ready to begin… and the program took off with an incredible bang of enthusiasm. I took each volunteer to one of the group homes that wanted to participate in the program — not all did — and, shakily, I introduced them to a potential "buddy" among the residents. It was very hard for me to make the visits and interact with the volunteers and the clients, but I seemed to be able to hold my agoraphobia and mental illness at bay.

For about two years the program was based in my home, but eventually a bigger space was needed. By this time, I had a co-coordinator, Thelma, helping me. She lived across the street and often I would find myself running across the road with an idea on my brain and a piece of paper in my hand. She would be waiting outside her apartment; she would also ford the roadway to my first-storey patio with ideas and questions.

Things changed once the program moved into an office in a medical building on the corner of Shelbourne and North Dairy streets. The office was about 40 minutes away by bus, and my agoraphobia would not allow me to continue. I worked in the office a few times, but my intense fear of having to be out of my home for great lengths of time led me to cope by using solvent, only a little at first. My "dry" period was over. After a few weeks I literally handed the program over to Thelma over my patio fence. I placed the bulk of the papers for the program — the ledger and all the brochures — in her hands, walked into my apartment defeated, and begin sniffing in earnest once again.

From that moment I had very little to do with the program, and the guilt of abandoning my dream consumed me. I dropped out of the CMHA and became a recluse. But the recreational and visiting program still runs today.

The program was a success, and brought me recognition and awards. The B.C. division of the CMHA named me volunteer of the year; an MLA gave me flowers on the Legislature steps during a mental health rally; CFAX, the leading local radio station, honoured me; and I was nominated for the prestigious Women of Distinction Award.

But the glory, once again, brought a surge in my mental illness. Though I had never intended being so front and centre in the public spotlight, I was. This attention, for some unknown reason, made me uncomfortable, even though all my life I had wanted to be noticed and successful. But success came with a price, and that was the loss of my anonymity. Neither my agoraphobia nor my difficulties talking to people made this success easy, and, just like at business school, I was embarrassed by all the attention.

The Women of Distinction Award was a major event in the city, with winners announced at a gala dinner. The night before the gala, I was in the psych unit at the Royal Jubilee Hospital. The event had created so much stress that I was suicidal, frightened and refusing to leave my home, and so, once again, was back in the hospital. It was a strange few days. The newspaper carried many articles and ads about this event, with photos and write-ups about the women, so keeping my nomination quiet was impossible. Staff on the ward congratulated me. I was, I suppose, successful, but felt unworthy.

The doctors released me to attend the banquet. But my embarrassment and terror did not allow me to enjoy the evening, and I rushed home to my apartment once the evening ended, getting stoned within minutes. Public life and the limelight were no longer for me. Reclusiveness became my lifestyle.

Things seemed to change after that. The supported independent living people distanced themselves from me because I was no longer a success story and was back using, staying by myself. I was chastised and shunned for my return to solvent; when the independent living workers did interact with me they were angry and judgmental. They felt I was no longer trying, and I sensed they wanted me out of this program. I felt I was a sore spot and made them feel inept. At the same time, I was assigned a case manager who seemed to have no interest in helping me. My loneliness pushed me to suicide attempts once again. Many of my friends tried to urge my caseworker to help, but she never responded to their concerns. In fact, she distanced herself even more. Life began to spiral quickly down and my self-hate was unbearable. I became so afraid to go out that my family, after many aborted invitations to dinner and outings, walked away from me. My sisters thought I was just choosing to stay home and sniff. They would not hear that I was trapped in my agoraphobia and was paralyzed with fear.

I was almost 50. And dramatic changes, once again, were coming.

25 MY WALK WITH GOD

I didn't relate to the diagnosis of bipolar disease. I thought everyone's life went up and down like mine. I figured I was just lazy when I was in the downward spiral, and enthusiastic when in the upward.

At the same time, I had the feeling that God made me suffer the torture of this unstable emotional dictatorship.

Things changed when I had Pat and Mike Piddington as friends. They made me feel like I had an "in" with God, finally. My relationship with Him was a little more stable than it had been. I rested in the knowledge that love was there for me, in quantity perhaps, somewhere in the universe. Some of this love was flowing through these two people to me.

My life revolved around the church more than ever before. I was there most Sundays, as that was where affection was to be found. My interest in God was a huge factor in keeping my life on track. I knew if I did good, God would reward me. And if I did badly, God would move away from me. This latter thought kept me sober, at least for a while.

My faith was childish, more than childlike. My vision of God's give-and-take quality was based on my childhood and the ups and downs of my unstable mother. If I did everything according to the perfectionistic expectations of my mother and God, I might be rewarded. If I didn't, I would be banished or punished in some manner. That had usually included the withdrawal of love and affection and being sent away — from home, to my room or to the basement — and told "I don't want to see you again until you're a better person."

I was always confused about God. My interactions with Him were a continuous cycle of banishment, acceptance, banishment — most often banishment. I would try to barter with God for rewards — happiness, success, love — by promising to do good deeds and have good thoughts.

However, I knew God would find me unacceptable. I stole. I am not sure anyone was fully aware of my pilfering adventures, but I would steal small things, like pills, stamps, sometimes small amounts of money and any available items, even if they really had no interest to me. I knew it was wrong, but I could not stop. It was a way — besides good grades — to stand out, even if it was for bad behaviour. I never got caught or, at least, no one ever said anything if they did know about it.

Even as a 10-year-old I would rifle through my mom's top bureau drawer. I was reading her mail, looking for confirmation that I was a good person. And helping myself to her Mellaril, which, I learned much later, was an antidepressant and antipsychotic. All I knew was that this little pill took the edge off my feelings. My hunt for information in her room often proved fruitless, yet I was sure people were talking about me behind my back. I just did not know what they were saying.

I later learned, while in prison, that this behaviour — breaching privacy and seeking attention, along with my suicidal ideations, led to my diagnosis of Borderline Personality Disorder. This label banished me to outsider status. Psychiatrists, general practitioners and everyone else who knew about Borderline Personality Disorder considered it incurable and people with my diagnosis were avoided and ignored. Any suicide threats and attempts were regarded as attention-seeking and not worthy of a response. I believed inside that I was terribly bad and there really was no option but to be alone. But I was very, very angry at the enforced isolation. Surely if God was a "good God" there would be gentle, loving care for me. There wasn't.

But, juxtaposed against this damnation, there was Pat. Somewhere an angel of mercy was watching over me. How could I, a sinner from the beginning of my church life at St. John's, "not worthy to gather up the crumbs under God's table," have hit a home run with such a caring, warm and desirable friend? Her opinion of me never seemed negative and I grew to love her deeply. Perhaps the caring and trust she bestowed upon me was the reason God took her from me only a few short years later. I was obviously being punished for having someone care.

My world revolved around me and my needs. While I was totally immersed in my world of pain, I don't remember really giving the needs of others much of a thought. Yet somehow I had been blessed with many, many friends, some who have remained friends for over four decades, supporting me through thick and thin. I had to be a worthy person, but I did not know how they came to know that. Was God easing up his iron grip on me? Was he allowing me to believe that I was a good person, at least at times? My hot and cold relationship with him became less of a trial and more of a peaceful interaction — at least for a while.

Years later, when my life began to stabilize and move forward in my mid-60s, I was repeatedly told that throughout this period I gave a lot of emotional support to people; that I was caring and a good listener; and that my constant efforts to better my life, though always plagued with the dips and peaks of my emotional and addictive world, were admired. Even though I felt I was going nowhere at all, I began to realize that maybe God really was looking after me.

But at the time when Pat and Mike were in my life there was a war between God and me, and I was determined to win, even though I did not know how. Why did I never walk away from this battle and push God away? Why did I continue to let my life revolve around a deity who seemed so punitive?

I believed that God would eventually save me and transform me into an angel. That was my hope.

26 NEIGHBOURS AND NEAR-DEATH

I'd gone to a very few lesbian drop-in groups in the '90s because I was afraid of my own "kind." I could not help but think being a lesbian meant that there was something terribly wrong with me. But I longed for companionship and people who would not judge me.

At one meeting, I developed a crush on a woman who seemed quite into the lesbian scene and knowledgable about lesbian activities — until I saw her aggressive behaviour towards the other women. At first I admired her spunk and what seemed to me to be strong self-confidence; however I soon noticed that she put down other women and attacked their sense of self-esteem with destructive words. I knew then that I wanted to avoid her at all costs.

And then one day in 1998, as I struggled with the success and pressures of the recreational and visiting program, she moved in next door to me in the Lampson Street apartment.

She became the most terrifying neighbour I had ever had. One day, early in her stay, I heard her yelling at and cursing some people in the apartment hall and I tried to step in and calm her down. She gnashed her teeth and lashed out at me, accusing me of interfering in a situation I knew nothing about and trying to put her down and embarrass her. All I had wanted to do was to calm things and end her verbal attack on those people.

After this, when she saw me in the hall or at my apartment door she would shriek, and stare at me with eyes oozing hate. I quivered and hung my head, terrified.

After a few months, a male friend of hers from Vancouver's Downtown Eastside of Vancouver moved in. At any time of the day or night, I could hear her swearing and screaming, lashing out at this man. More and more frequently, she would pound on my apartment door. Always more angry, always more combative.

And I began huffing more and more. My fear of her was so intense that I would not even go out onto my patio or through the door of my apartment.

I had become friendly with the woman who lived in the apartment above my neighbour. She kindly dropped her day-old newspapers onto my patio every morning, allowing me to have some contact with what was going on in the outside world even when I feared leaving my apartment. But, after a while, she became controlling, demanding I get sober.

As I sniffed more and more, both neighbours became more and more hostile. They probably feared me, as I feared them and their judgments. I now know that living in the same building with someone who was always intoxicated was intolerable to them, and they did not understand what I was going through. I also know now that I might have been able to stop the escalation of this hostility if I could have sobered up.

But I was desperate. I'd phone my angry neighbour, pleading with her to get medical help. I just wanted her to stop screaming and throwing things at her male friend.

And things became much worse, and much more frightening.

For almost all of 1999, my last year at Lampson Street, the neighbour would regularly phone the police and claim I was threatening to kill her. It wasn't true — in fact she had threatened my life several times and I found myself hiding away in my bedroom to get as far away from her as I could.

But each time she called, the police would arrive and cart me away to the emergency room at the Royal Jubilee Hospital. Once, when I was sitting with the police officer in Emergency, he told me he felt I was in danger of being severely hurt both physically and emotionally and that I needed protection from my neighbour, but also protection from myself. My using was causing me blackouts now, and I did not remember what I had been doing. I realized years later that I was most likely threatening to kill myself — partly to get away from my pain on Lampson Street, but also to find peace in this horrendous situation.

I don't think the police believed my neighbour, but they were concerned about me. The officers were gentle, respectful and always assured me that they would not hurt me, even though it seemed that whenever they came I was very intoxicated. These friendly men would wait with me in emergency, sometimes for hours and hours. They thought I would be admitted to the psychiatric ward under Section 22 of the Mental Health Act, which allows people to be held against their will for 48 hours if they're a danger to themselves or others. But, always, the doctors looked me over, harrumphed, and sent me back to my apartment.

And the next day, different police officers, again called by my neighbour, would knock on my door. I would be driven back to emergency, sit for hours in the waiting room and be sent home. The police continued to try and help me, even though there was no help to be had.

I finally realized that my sniffing, particularly the smell, was antagonizing all my neighbours and leading to the calls to police. I seemed to have had a very nasty relationship with many of them because of my addiction.

But I was in a trap. I needed both psychiatric help and help for my addiction. The mental health system would not work with psychiatric patients who had drug and alcohol problems. The drug and alcohol programs did not always extend services to clients with mental illnesses. Even in hospital, I felt I had fallen between the cracks.

Psychiatrists came and went — I'm sure I'd had almost every psychiatrist in the region by this time.

Still, I was treated well in the provincial alcohol and drug program, even as my sniffing continued to escalate. For a long time I had one-to-one counselling, but I would often be too intoxicated to show up, forgetting my appointments. For a while I attended groups, but they were useless to me because I was unable to talk. The drug and alcohol counsellors would recommend Narcotics Anonymous or Alcoholics Anonymous, but my agoraphobia and inability to speak in the meetings made attending these groups almost impossible — and in any case getting rides and finding sponsors was difficult.

I had tried Narcotics Anonymous years earlier, around 1975, and I did have a sponsor. Then she committed suicide. I was shattered yet again, and left wondering how these programs let someone down so much that they would kill themselves. Perhaps I should have continued on with NA, but perhaps I would have successfully committed suicide if I had. I didn't, because I was disgusted by the lack of support for my sponsor and I. There was nothing alcohol and drug workers, Narcotics Anonymous or Alcoholics Anonymous could do about my mental illnesses.

In the late 1990s, more and more people like me, with the dual diagnosis of addiction and mental illness, fell between the cracks of both systems, ultimately receiving very poor care.

Not only was I an addict, I also had bipolar and borderline personality disorders that made case managers and psychiatrists and even medical doctors give me a wide berth. As I had learned, people with Borderline Personality Disorder were considered incurable and manipulators of the systems. I felt totally alone and frightened, as I could no longer get even very poor care.

Kris Klusmeier and Brenda Macevicius of the Esquimalt Neighbourhood House, along with Jody Paterson, a journalist at the Victoria Times Colonist, had been trying to get the system to listen to my needs. On many occasions, holding their noses to be spared the smell of my place, they visited me. I was so distraught, and their caring was the only thing I had to hold onto. My family had more or less given up on me by this time. Even though I had many friends, they rarely visited because of the smell and my incoherent chatter.

Brenda, Kris and Jody sensed I had fallen between the cracks of the addiction and mental health programs, but they could find no one in either the medical system or the drug and alcohol system who would help me. These women realized that I had spent years unable to find appropriate help. I had been a revolving door client for both systems, as I always knew there really was no help for me, confirming my most terrifying fear — that I was just no good.

Even those who were supposed to help were making things worse. I dreaded visits to the psychiatrist I had in 2000 and 2001. He and my new, unresponsive case manager (an elderly woman who always seemed to be too busy to visit or even answer phone calls) would lay in wait for me. They would butt heads with me every time I arrived at the psychiatrist's office intoxicated. I was afraid of them, genuinely afraid, and once again fear led me to use more. I protected myself from being hurt by hostile and uncaring people with a shroud of solvent vapours. It might seem counterproductive, but I knew no other way to deal with hostility. I never could deal with or defuse anger, even as a child.

One day — the last day I visited this psychiatrist's office — I arrived, as usual, intoxicated. The doctor lashed out at me, with my case manager sitting smugly across from me. He berated me, peering down his nose at me with patriarchal authority, angrily letting me know that I was no good, that I would amount to nothing, and he had no more interest in being my doctor. I was told to get out of his office and out of the mental health centre.

I felt utterly powerless. I was horrified by his treatment of me and felt totally hopeless, totally defeated. Crying uncontrollably, I fled home, took a small overdose of Tylenol and was rushed to the emergency department by the police. This time, I was admitted to the psychiatric ward. When my psychiatrist came in the next morning, he discharged me without even talking to me. I was so angry and devastated that when I went home I began huffing once again. Waiting until I was totally numb from the solvent, I phoned the Esquimalt Neighbourhood House and told a staff member, as I continued to cry uncontrollably, what the psychiatrist had done. I could tell by her voice that she was horrified.

Minutes later I downed a whole bottle of Arthrotec that I had for my arthritis. I was on so many medications that I am sure they interacted with this massive dose. Within a few minutes I was staggering around my apartment, and then I remembered nothing until I woke up several days later in the respiratory ward of the Royal Jubilee Hospital, drifting in and out of consciousness, with no memory of how I got there.

I was later told that I was discovered laying, supposedly in a toluene stupor, in my apartment about two days after I had taken the pills. My upstairs neighbour had noticed I hadn't picked up the newspapers she left on my patio. Fearing something was wrong, she called the landlord and he, in turn, called the police. Officers found me face down in my bedroom. I was bleeding from a wound in my side; while convulsing from the effects of the pills I had fallen on a wooden divider that had splintered and pierced my skin.

The police thought I was just intoxicated and dragged me, unconscious, to the police car. Once they had taken me to the emergency department, the doctor realized I was unconscious from the overdose and he pumped my stomach. He recognized I had pneumonia from aspirating vomit as my body tried to get rid of the pills and moved me to the respiratory ward.

A few days later, one of the nurses told me they did not think I would pull through that first night.

When I was fully awake about six days later, Jody Paterson came to see me. She had been working on a newspaper article on me and the lack of co-operation between the drug and alcohol programs and the medical system which finally pushed me to attempt such a horrendous act.

The article hit the front page of the Times Colonist the next day — July 27, 2001. A few days later, I was committed to the psychiatric unit. The nurse greeting me made me dress in the hospital-issue pajamas and I was ordered to stay on the unit for my safety and to prevent me from running away.

The newspaper article, from the first day of admission to my last day there about six months later, was taped to the front of my nursing chart, a reminder that the treatment of dual-diagnosed people — and of me — might end up being exposed in the newspaper. Jody meant business.

As a result, I was assigned a new psychiatrist who was compassionate and very willing to work with me. However, I could not contain my anger at what had happened to me with my last psychiatrist, and at still being alive. Driven by my anger and hate, I often pushed the boundaries of the nursing staff by running away wearing only my pajamas, throwing things or threatening them. I truly did not care what I did. I was constantly suicidal and wanted only to be released. My return to life left only a bitter taste in my mouth.

I learned many years later, from a psych nurse who had been on a committee with representatives from both mental health and addictions several months after my discharge, that the two programs developed a plan to work together to deal with persons with dual diagnoses. I wonder to this day if this union came about because of the article that Jody Paterson had written. I do know, because this nurse told me, that my "falling through the cracks" had prompted these two systems to consider uniting.

I never went back to Lampson Street. The woman upstairs later told me that my angry next-door neighbour had abandoned her apartment and slunk away in the middle of the night. She was never heard of again around the lesbian circles of Victoria, so I presumed she had fled the city for somewhere up north where she had grown up.

After six months in the hospital, I was discharged. Still angry and still contemplating suicide, I wasn't convinced my hospitalization did any good.

However, while in the hospital, the ward psychologist began working with me on a dissociative identity behaviour I did not know I had, once known as multiple personality disorder.

I seemed to make some progress with her. No one had ever heard more than a snippet of my life until Dr. Lisa, the psychologist, began my therapy and some personalities began telling my story. I exhibited signs of multiple personality disorder — my life was being run, chaotically, by various "people" inside my body and brain. I couldn't remember what happened when they were in charge, which others often attributed to my addiction.

Dr. Lisa, after an intense first interview with me, realized that the fluctuating moods and behaviours she was witnessing did not fit my regular bipolar, borderline personality and addictive behaviour patterns. She asked my psychiatrist if she could investigate these incongruities. After a few sessions, she became aware that I was switching personalities, only a couple at first, but as time went by even more personalities came to the forefront and changes were more frequent. The conflict between these personalities was not only causing me to lose track of time, but also making me act oddly around other people. I often found myself struggling to explain why I was so belligerent or so passive, or unable to remember my behaviour when asked about it.

Later, after much counselling, instead of the personalities taking over I found myself lifting out of my body when talking to people who frightened me and watching from above. This seemed a safer place. Once the threat had retreated, I would return to my body.

Even today, this still happens. Now, though, I can recognize it, and move away from the trigger causing intense anxiety and return to my body, even while somewhat "threatened." I have made huge progress, but some perceived threats still trigger these dissociative spells.

Dr. Lisa was petite, gracious and regal, and I called her Princess. From the time I began working with her, I started to talk more fully about my past, a path that continued when I started counselling with the Women's Sexual Assault Centre. I began to recognize how the traumas led me to act the way I did all my life — addicted and frightened. My counsellor, Barb Peck, worked long and hard with me, taking me on for many extra sessions to help me sort out issues raised by the personalities. Finally, I began to feel that this last hospitalization had put me on a more healing track.

I left the hospital with my anger and a few possessions. I wanted to be discharged back in to the community and live on my own. But after searching for over a month, I could not find an apartment. There was only one I tried to rent, but I was turned down — partially because I was on disability pension and partially, I do believe, because of my history of addiction and mental illness. I could not afford to live in the community and landlords seemed to know that.

Instead, I was to go to a mental health apartment complex on Empress Street, a few blocks from my childhood home. I was horrified that at 50, and after 11 years of living independently, I was to be sent to another facility. My last days in hospital were spent sobbing uncontrollably.

Once again I was to become a full-time participant in the "psychiatric system."

27 EMPRESS STREET AND ART

While I was still in the psych ward, my case manager took me on a tour of the Empress Apartment, suggesting I might live there in supported housing. I was not impressed. The apartment I saw seemed like a lightless, almost uncivilized cave. There were no windows in the tiny bedroom. Even in prison, my cell had a small window.

The complex had two three-story buildings, one fronting on Bay Street and one on Empress Avenue. I toured the one on Bay, which was ugly, dark and noisy as ambulances and police cars travelled by on their way to the Royal Jubilee Hospital. I could never figure out how anyone could thrive in this place.

But I was more or less ordered to move into the apartments by the hospital administration. I was no longer in the acute stage of illness and the hospital wanted me out to make room for someone else who needed the bed.

I cried buckets in the days before. The fact was that no other housing in Victoria would have me because of my infamous addiction. I was relegated to this place. My case manager tried to win me over by pointing out there would be staff on duty around the clock who could keep an eye on me.

I ended up moving into an apartment in the Empress Avenue building, a wood and stucco 1950s apartment building with a basement suite, where I was placed.

On Christmas Eve, 2001, I left the hospital. My sister Joan had — not happily — stored my furniture while I was there. I was waiting in the apartment when the moving company, hired by the health authority, arrived. The basement was meant for two people, but I seemed to be the only one there. Streams and streams of belongings I hadn't seen in over six months spewed in the front door. The place was so large I would get exhausted walking from the living room to the bathroom and kitchen in the back. I was thrilled by the many cupboards and, most of all, by the walk-in closet in my cold, cement-walled bedroom. Somehow, before leaving Lampson Street I had collected more than 50 sweatshirts, and I was pleased that I had room to store many of them. This cupboard in my bedroom was also a great place to store my lacquer thinner.

With the couch and bed moved in, I decided to rummage around in my boxes for my Christmas tree. Finding a place to put it up was frustrating, as a brick planter ran through the middle of the living room. In the end I plunked it on a box and settled into watching it blink. The tree, only about three feet high, welcomed me to this very dismal place on Empress Street.

The apartment was dark, with small windows, and very cold even when I cranked up the thermostat. I would find myself sporting two or three of my 50 sweatshirts at any given time.

I followed my usual pattern in settling into a new place. Boxing Day found me at the Home Hardware on Cook Street, picking up my usual wares.

And once again I was alone. While in the hospital I had made friends with a woman called Beth, a blonde, middle-aged woman who usually wore denim overalls and T-shirts. She arrived at the hospital very thin indeed and left not quite so thin. Beth was outrageously funny and adventurous, loud and caring, always with energy to burn. I hung around her night and day because, as I always did in hospital, I felt so desperately alone and frightfully uninteresting. During all my many hospitalizations I tended to avoid conversations, or keep my responses minimal. When I did speak to people, I was so self-centred that no one really wanted to talk to me. I tended to be grumpy and stand-offish most of the time, which could be seen as shyness or being difficult. I always felt I had nothing to say, yet I wanted the attention of the nurses. People mostly avoided me, hoping to find a juicier conversationalist.

Beth pulled me out of this funk every time she drew near to me. Often we would get passes and go on short walks together. She became my way to overcome my fear, at least temporarily, of going outdoors. On Halloween night we strode confidently down to the fire hall in Oak Bay to watch the bonfire, eat hot dogs and popcorn. We stuffed ourselves with all the free food and oohed and wowed at the firework display. It happened to be a blue moon that night, the rare second full moon in a month, and we swooned under it, pretending we were ghosts and goblins among many of the children there to be judged for prizes for their costumes. Everyone seemed to get a prize and go off with a treat.

The evening I moved in to Empress Apartments, Beth and her husband brought me a huge bag of Christmas goodies and food. Their generosity blew me away. And they invited me to Christmas dinner the next day. As uncomfortable as I was sitting at the nicely decorated Christmas table, I was glad to be wanted. My sisters still were not talking to me and it had been a few years since I had even been in their homes. Special days were hard on me because I could only remember the good times that Anne, Joan and my dad shared with me in the past. Often I cried myself to sleep, wishing that I could get back into their good books — but that didn't seem like it would happen any time soon.

However, as all good things come to an end, the relationship between Beth and me dwindled away. Her illness and my illness were no longer compatible. Maybe our relationship cooled because outside the hospital I really felt I was no fun and no match for Beth's enthusiastic outlook and response to life. We had so little in common.

And my returning to using made interactions almost impossible, because I was quite often intoxicated whenever we met.

Beth had also gotten in trouble with the police — she had taken to setting fires in her apartment building and was eventually shipped away to the mainland for a while. The physical distance helped end our relationship, which had become unstable because of our personality differences — along with the fact that I had written a scathing note to her husband urging him to leave her because her illness just meant trouble. For some reason Beth took offence at this!

I just wanted him to be safe. In prison at Colony Farm, a fellow inmate was an arsonist who mainly set fires when she was sexually aroused. After being jilted by a man at a community dance, she almost set the day area on fire. We were saved but I was frightened. I just did not want this to happen to Beth's husband.

Meanwhile, I was settling in to my apartment, putting everything away. And then the Empress team leader — a nurse who managed the staff and life in our complex — told me I was moving to a single apartment upstairs, and I needed to pack up.

I was more than annoyed, because even though I was told I would get help to pack, I never did. It didn't occur to me until years later that my sniffing kept help from happening. I was left in peace to sniff and wrap and box… angry and dejected.

The moving company transported all my stuff up 12 outside stairs to the single-occupancy suite upstairs. It was rather big, with a large, dark living room that was one step up from the front door. My bedroom, facing south and streamed in sunlight, was located across a tiny hall from the entrance. The most important place was the bathroom, a long, narrow space with a huge floor to ceiling window. Sunlight seemed always to stream in here as well. I spent a lot of time in the bathroom flushing Kleenex down the toilet with the aim of stopping snorting for a few days or forever. But I just could not seem to fulfil my half-hearted dreams, and would soon wad up tissue to begin the ritual of sniffing all over again.

The apartment had just two closets, one in my bedroom and one, a pantry-style closet, just off the bathroom. I had to part with my 50 sweatshirts! Somehow I managed, though, throughout my time at Empress, to make huge donations to Big Brothers and Sisters — clothes and other items I needed to shed to keep those closets from bursting at the seams.

I was given help from the staff to unpack. I was sober that day, I suppose. Somehow, within a couple of hours, the place became a semblance of home. Still, I was angry that I was here at Empress and not out in the community. This rage, for it was rage, hung with me for over three years. I fought tooth and nail to reject this place yet, three years later, after a few suicide attempts, some more serious than others, I was asked if I really wanted to live there and, after being told I would end up on the street if I left, I decided to quit resisting and become part of the community.

Life at Empress was not totally uncomfortable and unacceptable. Many of the staff, particularly Thelma Williams, a support worker, made life a bit more bearable. She was kind, and not deterred by any state of sobriety I was in. She helped out, carrying groceries, making beds, cleaning up my kitchen and just being there to show undying support. I came to love her for her sweet generosity of spirit. Also, the Empress held Christmas and Easter dinners in the Common Area just below my apartment, and we had summer barbecues every year. Hot dogs and burgers never tasted so good, and the smell of charcoal on my clothes gave me a more respectable odour. I enjoyed eating and drinking with the group just a little, I must admit. The gatherings lasted as long as the food was present. Then the numbers of clients dwindled quickly as people returned to their rooms. Lots of prep time; not so long on the eat time.

We residents were a mishmash of age, mental health problems and social skills. Most of the tenants were very ill, some taking to talking to themselves and enjoying their own company; some quiet and withdrawn. Many of us also had drug and/or alcohol problems — most of them had kicked their habits — and most were smokers. Many hung around the Common Room, next to the office, to watch TV, mingle or just plain annoy the staff. Except when I had to go down for my medications, which were doled out to me four times a day, I rarely took advantage of the common area — mostly because I was unwelcome due largely to my usual stench. (Eventually a sign was posted near the office to advise tenants not to wear perfume or other scents in the common area or office. Only recently did I realize this sign was meant for me. I never did pay attention to it.)

I created a garden on the 12 outside steps up to the apartment. Some 20 pots of flowers brought attention to the positive in my life at the Empress. Yet there was a huge problem with my apartment inside — the step up and down between rooms was a tripping hazard and I was always falling, crashing into the wall or my shelves of collectables arranged near the stairs in my living room. Not only was I risking breaking my head open, I seemed to smash everything in the way of my head. Falling was a regular thing for me; I even split my head after tripping and crashing into the coffee table. Most often I was stoned, though I even fell when I wasn't. I was sensitive to medications and some caused me to lose my balance even when I was not using.

My moods escalated. Depressions were deep. Manias were high. Psychosis was rampant.

I tended to stay alone in my apartment, and though I was blessed with many friends outside the complex, I felt lonely. Still, I did not invite anyone else from the Empress Street complex up to talk or visit. There was, in my mind, no one of the same intellectual ability as me, so I wanted to be left alone.

The hugeness of my place made making it cozy difficult. After a while, I just settled for pulling a chair to the front window and watching everyone on the block. I started buying solvent from the local hardware store in gallon sizes so that I wouldn't run out. The police, when they had been called repeatedly to deal with me intoxicated, ended those purchases two or three years into my tenancy when they reported me to the hardware store and told them not to sell me any more solvent. The Empress staff, I later found out, had been advised not to deal with me when I was intoxicated and to call the police.

After this, I cringed anytime I tried to buy solvent at any store. I waited a few months before I returned to the Home Hardware and pretended, in my mind, that I was a house builder who needed to buy the solvent for whatever it was actually used for. I was desperate because I had already been banned by one store downtown, and now another had put me on its do-not-sell list. I had only two other places to buy. Hard times had truly begun.

Yet I started to feel hope. When the team leader breezed in, though not pleased with my solvent addiction, she whisked by me in the day room and often said, with an air of hope, that my efforts to find sobriety were just "progression before perfection." The nurse's statement seemed to prod me on. I was starting to feel that perhaps there was hope for me in winning a lasting sobriety. She made me feel that I was not being condemned for my huffing, but rather being offered support in my efforts to find a different way of life. As time went along I began to stay sober, for a few days at first, then for a month or two, and finally for a year or two as well.

Quite honestly, I still wanted to perfect my using, not my sobriety.

Somewhere in all of this, my mind started playing tricks on me. Blackouts, which had plagued me from time to time during my huffing history, became more and more frequent. I would lose many hours, days and even months where I would not know what I was doing or where I was. Now I realize some of the blackouts were a result of the dissociative disorder, while others were definitely caused by the solvent. At the time, I just thought that these blackouts were just due to my using.

Around my fifth year at Empress, I began to keep watch from my window, spying on the lady who lived in a white 1950s house across the street. In the front of her property was a white picket fence and a trellis that was covered in roses in the summer. All hours of the day and early evenings she was out in her front yard digging, pruning and just looking over her piece of Eden. While watching her, day after day, I started to realize that she had killed her husband and buried him in the front yard. I felt she was trying to cover up this desperate act by planting flowers and bulbs. I kept phoning the police to have her arrested and, for the first few times, officers came to get my story, but they never arrested her. The police, however, seemed to be getting more annoyed at me.

The staff at Empress kept telling me, then demanding, that I stay away from the window. Finally, after a great dressing-down, I decided to go about my business and leave the lady alone. I still continued to be convinced of the murder but lost interest in this whole drama once she finally moved out.

Then I began to believe that people were going to kill me. At first these thoughts were random and occasional, but, as time went along, they became more and more frequent. I never was sure where the thoughts originated. I was so frightened that I started packing a knife, also keeping one ready to grab near the front door. Believing that my place was bugged, I would only answer the phone in my bedroom, not the living room. I was so scared that I would lash out verbally with staff and my new case manager, Hayley Porteous. I would also write letters and notes to staff and tenants, trying to protect myself from harm; these caused no end of problems. I also wrote long, feverish emails to my dad trying to analyze his part in my formative years and his relationship with my mother. I found out later he just began to ignore my epistles and finally erased the messages from his inbox when my "psychiatric advice" came flooding in.

My using escalated. And then, well into my fourth year at Empress, I ceased using once or twice for many, many months.

My life settled down a bit. I went to support groups run by the drug and alcohol program and by USTAT (Urgent Short Term Assessment and Treatment), mainly on depression. I had, more or less, returned to the drug and alcohol offices of my own volition. Being desperate for positive attention from the Empress staff, I was willing to work on my addiction. I was also enrolled in a group for people who were still using but practising harm reduction. This program made it easier for me to accept my limitations in attaining sobriety yet, at the same time, gave me motivation to try.

My psychiatrist recognized that dealing with my depression was a key element in my recovery. My case manager referred me to a few groups on depression management. For once, I found the groups helpful. I started to understand that a lot of my addiction was a way to cope with my depression (and mania), and began to listen to and practise mindfulness exercises — a kind of meditation to centre oneself in the present when under duress that is also useful in day-to-day life. I learned how depression affects the mind and body. It was a 10-week program, with a two-and-a-half hour session each week. We made weekly goals that I began, with great vigour, to practice. Life for me started to become a little less dramatic and more peaceful as a result.

I eventually tried small group therapy programs, but my inability to talk made me uncomfortable, and they were mostly useless for me.

But my life really started to change when I enrolled in a dialectical behaviour therapy program meant specifically for people with Borderline Personality Disorder. I attended once a week for a year. A counsellor from the drug and alcohol program had recommended the therapy, putting in a referral for me. When I was accepted, I hunkered down for the long haul. My life began to change and to have meaning. My borderline behaviour took a turn for better as I began to understand how to communicate with others — and how not to — and make mindful decisions about how and what to say and not say. I was shown ways to live my life with less drama and more foresight. I thrived in this class and made it through the whole year without using — and missed only one session due to illness. My Borderline Personality Disorder traits were slowly disintegrating. However, I ran into one of my common problems in this program — I felt stupid. I would zone out, as the saying goes, and even though I was aware of everything that was said in class, I was rendered speechless when asked a question, sounding like I wasn't paying attention.

The dialectical behaviour therapy program, through specific exercises and the therapeutic model of cognitive behaviour therapy, taught me the effects of emotions and thoughts on my actions, and things began to make sense to me. I was introduced to a way of thinking that did not include just "black and white thoughts" —

something being either good or bad — which was a pattern most people with Borderline Personality Disorder had. There were grey areas as well. I learned I could have mastery over my thoughts and emotions by learning to change the way I thought about a situation. Knowing that I could change negative thoughts and behaviours into something more pleasant gave me incentive to really try hard in this program. I did not want the drama in my life any more. I wanted peace and control.

The facilitators of the program were delightfully amiable and patient with the 10 participants. We all struggled. Mastery, or even something close to mastery, was so difficult. As I had found in many programs, self-criticism and doubt plagued me. Facing these demons head on, without using, seemed an insurmountable task. Yet I was determined to understand. More determined to change. I really do not know why this program had such an inspiring effect on me, except perhaps I was now ready to change. Why? I think the programs at USTAT and drug and alcohol had set me on the trail to make these changes.

One of the counsellors in the dialectical behaviour therapy program realized during an interview that I was prone to anxiety, especially social anxiety. After I finished the behaviour therapy program, she registered me in a social anxiety course at the mental health centre. This course turned out to be the best and most helpful program I had ever taken. That is saying a lot, because the depression program and dialectical behaviour therapy were incredibly helpful too.

After the social anxiety course, conversation seemed easier and, for a while, ceased to be a problem. Learning that I did not have to talk to everyone I met, and that everyone did not require the same level of interactions — talking with a stranger only required small talk, but conversation with friends and family could be a little more intimate and revealing — I began to converse more with anyone, anywhere. My confidence swelled and my inhibitions dwindled. I never realized that my poor communication skills were the result of this anxiety. I was set free of my own bondage.

Probably for the first time, I realized I wasn't stupid or uninteresting. I considered myself "stupid" if I didn't know about a topic that came up in conversation. But the course helped me realize that even though I might know nothing about the topic at hand, I knew a lot about a lot of things. This knowledge that I really wasn't so dumb truly freed me.

The other key in this program was the idea that I could rate my anxiety levels before and after conversations and activities. I found that I was often more anxious before a conversation than I was after. I began to realize I could talk to people and did not have to reveal anything really personal about myself. Though I never got terribly good at it, I could produce small talk. Slowly I was coming out of my rabbit hole and starting to live my life in a new way.

After four or five years at Empress, I started attending Laurel House, a drop-in centre for persons suffering from mental illness located on Elford Street. It was in a large turn-of-the-century three-story house with an art studio in a separate, more modern building next door. My case manager, again in her wisdom, referred me to this program.

At first I was hesitant to go because it meant I had to be sober for the day. My attendance was inconsistent because I just could not seem to make headway into getting to know the other participants. I eventually hooked up with the art department. I started out with the pottery classes, but soon lost interest as I quickly made too many warped and ugly pots, ornaments and other miscellaneous, unrecognizable items to fit into my apartment. My friends were hesitant to receive these as offerings of appreciation.

When my spirit wandered from the clay department, the program facilitator, Susan, encouraged me to try painting. I told her adamantly that I could not paint. But I learned quickly that I had a small talent, though I was embarrassed by being in the same space as more advanced artists. I felt very inhibited indeed. But, I persevered. The instructor, though never giving her opinion of my work (or anyone else's for that matter), kept encouraging me to work on other pieces. My fascination with what my paintbrush could do propelled me into a new and exciting way of life. I could express myself, mainly through creating landscapes, and I now had something to talk to people about.

Art became a way of life; a transporter of dreams; a lifeline to sanity. I found comfort in landscapes and splattered the canvas with acrylic paint. I didn't totally appreciate my work, but other people did — with gusto. Despite my uncertainties, I continued, self-taught, experimenting with myriad techniques, brushes and colour combinations, and my work started gaining a sense of polish. I had opened the door to a new, much more acceptable career than secretarial work ever was. My sister, in her wisdom, took me to Opus Art Supplies on Herald Street and invested about $500 in paints, canvases and brushes for me to do art at home. Sober and not so sober, I began painting regularly, producing some quite acceptable pieces. I found quickly that when I was using, I could create profound pieces in the first hour, but as the time dragged on I just wasted paint and canvasses as I sank into the black space of vapour fog. Nonetheless, I persevered with painting. This really was my calling, I felt.

At first I just hung my art in the Common Room. I sold the occasional piece, but did not yet think my work was up to saleable snuff. My little studio, tucked into the end of my living room, was rather dark with little lighting, but it was the hub of my new activity. I was thrilled to have something to do besides watch out the window of my apartment. I had a purpose. I could form a dream of a new life for the very first time. I was liberated.

When Laurel House was closed in 2008 due to funding cuts and a new direction taken for drop-in centres for mental health clients, my little studio became my lifeline to sanity.

Eventually I began to make a name for myself as an artist. The Vancouver Island Health Authority — now Island Health — had an art program, run by Fatima McCarthy, called Art Capacity. I immediately got involved in some of their programs, first just by observing when it came into the Empress Apartment, then by participating in the fun every Wednesday afternoon. Eventually Fatima encouraged me to show my art at various functions around town. I was among a selection of artists invited to display and sell work as part of a fundraiser at the Edelweiss Club where Louise Rose, a local favourite singer, performed that night. I sold my first publicly displayed painting, and I was ecstatic. As embarrassed and apologetic as I was displaying my work, many people seemed to enjoy my rather childlike portrayals of the world around me.

Fatima also encouraged me to make cards of my art to, as she put it, obtain "seed money." I eagerly took photographs of my paintings and trucked down to London Drugs to have copies made. I pasted the photos onto card stock and over the years have sold many hundreds, perhaps even thousands, of cards in my continuing career — all because Fatima seemed to see something in me that I could not yet see.

Even today I still paint, holding an art show once a year at the Eric Martin Pavilion. I sell a lot of paintings and cards. Art has given me a little extra income — pocket money — that I never had before.

And art will be with me until the end of my time thanks to Susan at Laurel House and Fatima with Art Capacity.

Through all the turbulence in my life, others were with me, friends who never gave up on me — Claudia D; Joan S; Sandra; Ann M; Susan G; Norma K; Jody P; Barbara H; Dr. C; and the Fyles. I had strong believers in my potential and my goodness, even while I had a wild addiction and an uncontrolled bipolar disorder. Their support eventually led me to a wholeness I never could have dreamed of, a chance to experience life in its fullness. I thank all these friends and many, many more. A simple thank you is such a frail gesture to fully encompass my feelings of joy and hope; something they all endowed me with.

My life at Empress, though still in the throes of chaos, was changing. My understanding of my illnesses was becoming more concrete, and I was becoming closer to wholeness.

I was starting to strive, and I was beginning to thrive!

28 HAYLEY PORTEOUS

I had not had much luck with case managers. During my time on Lampson Street and in my early years at Empress, my case manager seemed to give up on me. Her main roles were to keep a watchful eye and prevent me from harming myself and guide me into programs within the mental health system. She did very little of either. She just was not interested, or so it seemed, in me or my plight in life. She was never available to answer phone calls from my friends or me and rarely came to see me at home. I never saw her at the office except on the rare occasions I had a psychiatrist's appointment. Still, during my second or third year at Empress, I managed to remain sober for a whole year. My case manager insisted on taking take me out for lunch in Sidney, at a restaurant on the harbour, to celebrate. We celebrated in style. The next day I went back to using — in my focus on staying clean for a year, I didn't make plans to maintain my sobriety. I was so lost the next day that using was the only way I could find myself again. Once again, I defeated myself.

After several other short-term case managers, I was eventually paired with Hayley Porteous. Pixie-like, with an impish smile, she was just out of university with a social work degree when I met her 10 years ago. I was probably the most challenging case to test her new skills.

Hayley came into my life when I lived in the Empress Apartments. She treated me creatively and tenderly from the beginning. She walked that extra mile — or two — as she tried to make sense of my ups and downs, my suicidal thoughts and actions, my solvent abuse and my mental illness in its full-blown glory. She seemed, over time, to deeply care about me and my future. Never once did she manipulate me to do what she wanted; she always seemed to know what I needed and encouraged me to embrace my life and my days with confidence and hope. Even though I had neither confidence nor hope when she arrived on the scene, I began to gain them. She cried with me, never fought with me, laughed with me and journeyed with me.

I had experienced several wonderful people in my life by this time. But no one like Hayley. She would drive me to the hospital when I was sick, whether from the solvent or illness. She never gave up on me, though many years later she tearfully told me that every time she left me ,she wondered if would ever see me again — except perhaps at my funeral.

Her attention and caring kept me going through the bleakest moments of my life. She would talk me down from my ever more extreme manic highs, walk with me as I climbed out of deep, cavernous lows, and fight for me in the mental health system. I knew I had a friend and reliable person to journey with me in my life.

Hayley introduced me to the courses that brought change. She saw great potential in me and allowed me to take steps — very small ones at first — towards my independence of soul. She stuck with me for over 10 years through thick and thin — walked my path, cried in my pain, rejoiced in my victories and encouraged me, over and over and over again. I was being guided by an angel.

And because of her undying faith in me, I started to change.

I was hospitalized many, many times while Hayley was my case manager. She was always moved to tears when I spoke of or attempted suicide. Yet never once did she judge me. I made the same mistakes over and over, with small variations, and she was there with compassion and patience. Hayley didn't yell or bully me, but she did treat me as a human being and not an object requiring pussyfooting.

Even when my behaviours did not seem to change, she never gave up on me or threatened to leave. She never played God. I wasn't shunned or chided for my behaviours. Instead she helped me, little by little, to overcome those habits that frustrated and angered other folks — manipulation, passive aggressiveness, solvent abuse and just plain forgetfulness of what I was trying to accomplish.

And she never told me to stop using.

For all these things, I began to love her, for I knew I was in the hands of love.

On my desk today I have a cherished photo Hayley gave me at Christmas the first year she was my case manager. On her right arm is tattooed "This tornado loves you." I thought she was making advances on me. However when I timidly asked if this was true, she quietly said "No." It was a quote from a book she had read and she felt compelled to have it on her arm, she said. Now I notice she covers up her arm, and I wonder if she regrets the tattoo. She might regret it, but I don't. For I know this tornado loves me!

I owe Hayley my life. I still struggle with suicidal thoughts, depression, some mania, but I have much more control and I am sober. If I spoke of suicide in those days, her eyes welled up with tears. But she didn't say "I don't want to hear this again." She said she was there for me, I was free to make my own decisions and she would be at my funeral. "I will be there for you."

I have never tried to harm Hayley, physically or emotionally, something that I often tried with others who reached out to help me or got too close to me because I did not know how to handle intimacy in any form. When I spoke to Hayley, I was honest and not manipulative. She was the same.

Who else in this world treated me this way? Only Pat Piddington and the Fyles, perhaps.

I am the luckiest person alive to have had her as my case manager and friend — her unselfish leadership has helped make me who I am today.

In 2017, Hayley, near the end of her studies for her master of social work, accepted a new position in another part of the system. As I hugged her goodbye, I wished her blessings and told her she was my hero.

Hayley stood outside my apartment door, tears in her eyes.

"Don't ever forget it — YOU are MY hero," she said.

I have been blessed.

29 ROCKLAND APARTMENTS

As 2012 rolled around, I faced a new challenge — moving from Empress Street.

To me, it seemed like I had just moved in, when in fact I had been there almost twelve years. The staff at Empress were concerned that I would fall down the steps to my apartment and be seriously injured. They wanted security for me because I still was suicidal a lot of the time and they felt I still needed a place that would offer some support when life became rough. But they also thought I was ready for more independence.

Many of my former case managers had been looking for a new, secure and more permanent apartment for me. They were hoping for a ground-level suite — no stairs — with room for an art studio and my fish. After a year of intense looking, they found one in an Island Health apartment building called Rockland. I didn't want to move. Moving felt sudden, rushed. But on March 20, 2012, after a month of packing — usually between midnight and 3 a.m. — I moved. I had so much stuff that I filled a small U-Haul trailer to the brim. As I packed, I was surrounded by a fortress of boxes. Often I found myself throwing my belongings into boxes, only sometimes taking the opportunity to wrap up breakable items. I was overwhelmed by the task, and I resented having to do the packing all alone once again.

Once again, I didn't recognize then that the reason no one was helping me was because I would stop and have a sniff every now and then as I slowly packed my belongings.

By some miracle I had quit sniffing solvent, yet again, a week before I was relocated. This time I was determined, mostly out of shame, that I would never let the tenants of my new place know that I was a huffer. I had been humiliated enough by my addiction, and this time I would get a handle on it.

Not only was I ashamed, but the nurse at Rockland threatened to send me out of my apartment each time I used, warning that I would not be able to return for eight hours. I knew, and my case manager Hayley knew, that I had nowhere I could go except downtown, and my legs, which were weak and so painful when walking, could not stand wandering aimlessly around downtown for eight hours. The threat of being sent away from home for that length of time motivated me even more to stay sober.

When the day arrived, the moving men came in waves, bringing my furniture and belongings into this new, somewhat brighter, home. I had so much stuff the movers did not know where to put it all, so it was stacked in huge piles in the living room. Fortunately, I had two wonderful friends, Susan Gage and Louise Crumrine, come that day to help me organize and unpack the bedroom and kitchen. These angelic folks helped me arrange and re-arrange my living room and art area, moving the unpacked boxes and furniture until there was a sense of order. Having two unpacked rooms comforted me — I could at least go to sleep and eat in relative peace. My friends had done a huge part of the work and I felt so blessed with their help.

For the next three days, day and night, I continued unpacking. When I was at Empress Street, I had done a lot of downsizing, knowing that I wouldn't have room for everything in my new digs. But I still had too many possessions. The downsizing continued as I attempted to find a place to put everything.

My art area, part of the living room, evolved. It was bigger than I had at Empress. At first I worried that, being right by the door, it would be the first area greeting my guests as they walked in. So I made a note to keep the area as tidy as possible, yet functional at the same time. I managed over the years to do both, much to the amazement of many of my guests.

Past the art corner was the living room, serene and inviting. I had two goldfish at Empress Street. My sister Anne took on the task of relocating them; on the second day she brought around my pets in a bucket of water and also my 30-gallon tank. After a successful transfer of my "family" into their relocated home, my living room was complete. I was ecstatic being reunited with the loves of my life. A moment of peace prevailed.

For the previous seven or eight years, I had been allowed to have fish at Empress, despite the health authority's ban on pets in the apartments under their control. I think the higher ups realized that these underwater pets brought a calm and a purpose to my life. I took care of them, talked with them, told stories to them and generally adopted them as one would a dog or cat. They helped resolve, to a great degree, one of my most disabling fears — loneliness. Having something alive in my place, and, reflecting back on the piranhas that I had shared with Betty back in the '70's, made me feel so much less isolated.

Since that time on Empress, fish have been constant companions. Despite deaths — and I do mourn them, as do the fish left behind — I carry on raising them. They are my companions, my family. Without the Rockland staff person, Jennifer, and my friend Patricia Kyffin, I would not be able to keep the tank clean or my fish healthy. Lifting pails of water or trying to vacuum the bottom of the tank was often too difficult for me, because I have very little strength in my upper body and need a walker or cane to get around safely when carrying heavy objects. These two women gladly help me out.

I would be more isolated than ever if ever I had to relinquish my companions. They are a tremendous and vital part of my life.

Three days of almost constant unpacking brought me closer to completing my move. But it also left me totally exhausted and very emotionally charged. I was manic and scared at the same time, aware that I was in danger of returning to my solvent. I never did, yet somehow I ended up in the Psychiatric Emergency Services at the Royal Jubilee Hospital once again. I was too tired and too overwrought to even care what happened to me, and I suspect my case manager decided I needed a rest.

There were three or four beds, all occupied, so I spent several nights sleeping in a reclining chair in a common area. Psychiatric Emergency Services, though a step up from the lock-up units in Eric Martin Pavilion, was not a great place to be. Most often, after being interviewed by a staff member and the psychiatrist on duty (and they were brutal and seemingly did not care what happened or what would happen to the person), I, though feeling so much in need of safe and supportive care, would be discharged. So often, this kind of care was simply not available. Sending people home with a pamphlet outlining services such as the inaccessible detox or programs such as AA, NA or the Umbrella Society seemed such a cold, uncaring blow to those who really needed help.

I never found Psychiatric Emergency Services helpful. For one thing, there were not enough treatment beds, so most of the patients slept on lazy boy chairs until, after some renovations, some cozy leather chairs that could be pulled out to make a bed were added. Once in a while I found myself sleeping on a gurney in the back hallway. This was, to be sure, very, very uncomfortable and I could not easily get on and off — I was too short and the bed moved when I tried to leap up on it.

The general treatment on this ward consisted of occasionally being given an Ativan (a minor tranquilizer). No talking therapy. Psychiatric Emergency Services would not allow iPods or Walkmans or cell phones. There was nothing to do all day except watch TV, with no sound — instead "the inmates" watched the closed captions that flashed along the bottom of the screen. No forms of mental stimulation were allowed, so we all sat in bored silence during our stay.

Some of the "inmates" were lucky enough to have visitors to pass the day. Most often no one came to visit me, except my case manager each morning.

The question I asked myself often was "why do I always end up here — there is absolutely no help to be had."

I knew it was just a holding tank for folks whose life seemed unmanageable. We all knew we would be turfed, the sooner the better, with no therapy or supports except for a few pamphlets and phone numbers and a drug prescription.

After four days, I was discharged.

And the embarrassed Rockland staff realized they hadn't know I was gone.

One of the stipulations of my residency at Rockland was that my medications would be given to me from the office four times a day. Even though I hadn't shown up for days to pick up my meds, I was told later, the staff just thought I was sleeping, having exhausted myself with the move.

Still, I've grown to know and trust them, and the Rockland staff treat me with respect. There's a nurse and team leader, and staff working day, evening and night shifts. Often the nurse will take clients to medical appointments, but for the most part I am able to make my way to doctor and other appointments without any assistance. The staff daily hands out medications to some of the more than 40 people in two buildings here at Rockland. Some, like me, are at times actively suicidal, and others, also like me, just can't handle their own meds safely.

I find the staff supportive and, most often, easy to talk to. Knowing that I can be straight up with them in conversation helps me to make decisions about whether I need to see my psychiatrist or case manager or to just hang in and deal with difficult situations on my own. I am often given Ativan when my world gets out of whack — too fast, too depressed, too anxious. I feel, with all my mood swings, safe here.

It hasn't all been a smooth ride. I have had many swipes with suicide, one putting me into the psychiatric unit of the Royal Jubilee Hospital in 2015 for 11 days. A very deep and insurmountable depression had settled on me that lasted over a year. I had isolated myself for most of that time and, so tired of trying to manage just the simple day to day chores and errands, I felt very lost and without hope. I felt paralyzed by my life and was certainly not experiencing pleasure at any level. So I knew that my time had come to say "good-bye" to Planet Earth. I was very much on the verge of killing myself when I was discovered. I had all the pills (more than 500 Tylenol) lined up on my kitchen counter. I was contemplating swallowing them when I was interrupted by a relief staff person because I'd sent a casual email to Hayley, my case manager, and something triggered her to phone Rockland and ask them to check on me.

That was my last hospitalization. I had never dreamed I could stay out of the hospital. I was known in the mental health community as the person with the most hospital days, and this was one of the reasons I was moved to Rockland. The health authority hoped that providing security and independence would end the hospital revolving-door syndrome. Even though I did have a few trips to Psychiatric Emergency Services during the first four years of my stay, I gained confidence in my mental health and addiction recovery, so fewer and fewer trips were needed. Now I am hospital-sober!

My moods still continued to swing during my first four years at Rockland. I was on medication to control the "over-the-top" mania, but still would get manic on a regular basis, and then, after the mania subsided, I would dip into deep, dark depressions. When I was manic I would usually cease to eat and sleep. Most of the time I would fill my social and daily calendar with endless, almost impossible to keep, appointments and activities. And yes, I did keep them — at least at first. As I got higher and higher, going faster and faster, spending money as though I had a million dollars (I didn't), I was unable to focus on anything and began thinking I was God's gift to a world that needed to be "saved." Each time, I spiralled out of control eventually. What initially was fun became emotionally painful — I could not keep up to myself. My speech, pressured and fast, often alerted friends or the staff that I was heading to a crash that would bring another depression.

I still am being treated by a psychiatrist in the mental health system. As my moods keep on swinging, my medications keep on being adjusted; at one point almost every time I visited a previous psychiatrist he seemed to make changes to my drug regime. Not only were my medications always being adjusted, my psychiatrists also changed frequently during my years at Empress and Rockland, because they all tended to move on to work in different areas of the system. Some stayed for a few years, some for a few months. I became almost immune to their help because I never really wanted to depend on them to be there when I needed them. I always sensed that they would move on — and they always did, probably from the results of burnout.

I'm still at Rockland six years later — and I have never huffed once. I was determined not to use, and I never have. I was able to keep my addiction quiet — even now none of the residents know about my addiction history, only the staff.

I have rarely felt alone here. Throughout my stay I have gotten to know and respect almost everyone, and everyone has gotten to know, trust and respect me. I feel like their elder. There were a couple of young men who seemed to look up to me like I was a mother. Never in my life had I dreamed I would be in a position where caring and dialogue would be so important, or that I would take on such a critical task as a mothering role.

There have been tense moments in the last year. All the Rockland residents were told in October 2017 that we would be evicted by July 1, 2018. The health authority assured us we would not be homeless, but we had no idea where we would be going. Despite the upset, I seemed to hold back my own emotions, wanting more than anything to be sure that any new place would have space for both my fish and my art studio.

I decided to try not to think of our eviction until after Christmas, and mostly stuck to my guns. But I threw out millions of prayers, reaching out to God, asking that we get a reprieve of a couple of years. I did believe we would be allowed to stay, but when Christmas was over, the worrying and uncertainty became a source of panic for me. I obsessed over this unstable situation and finally ended up in Psychiatric Emergency Services overnight once again. But once the panic subsided with a small dose of Ativan, I returned home the next morning. Continually praying that we could stay at Rockland became a frantic, obsessive pastime.

And in March, Island Health announced an agreement with the landlord that would allow I and some other residents to stay in Rockland — now called Sorona — for another 2.5 years. (Some tenants, in the meantime, had moved to market housing, with a rent subsidy; others moved to places with more intensive supports.) Not only that, the building is being upgraded, including balconies that you can actually sit on (the old ones were unsafe); better lighting outdoors and in the hallways; and a newly landscaped yard with flower beds and trees the previously neglected property. I am so delighted to be able to enjoy these changes that I have even begun to upgrade my apartment, making it more cheery and uncluttered.

I have never felt more relieved than I did getting this reprieve from having to move immediately. Because Rockland is centrally located, I can get around with my "four-wheel drive" (my walker) relatively easily both in the neighbourhood and downtown. Rockland Apartments is quite close to the Oak Bay Junction and its stores. Because I have been spoiled by this convenience, I am hoping that the next move will take me to a centrally located part of the city.

Thank you, Island Health and Lantern Properties: you have brought back security to all of us who remain.

Early in 2017, I began treatment for anxiety. My psychiatrist told me that, most often, people who had addiction issues were wrought with anxieties, and once the anxieties were addressed and treated, the addiction lessened or disappeared. Even though the principles I learned from the social anxiety group program I had attended while at Empress worked for quite a while, the terror of interacting with strangers, and even new friends, returned. I always needed reassurance that I was not speaking out of turn and offending someone.

As I gained more and more sobriety, my anxieties increased. I realized that my past using was a way of coping with my agoraphobia and fear of dealing with other people. I was missing this buffer.

My anxiety increased so much so that I was sleepwalking, losing track of time, afraid to go out alone, afraid to spend an evening with myself. I began to go to bed at 5 p.m. and get up in the middle of the night to paint — art had become a major part of my life. I hid away from the outside world. Art had become my new "using."

By 2015 — my third year in Rockland — trying new activities had become harder and harder. My apartment, once again, had begun to feel like a prison, a feeling that continued until early in 2016 when I was prescribed a new drug to help control the disabling effects of my fears.

In the mental health system, drugs are a constant. I was prescribed Loxapine for my severe and disabling anxiety, but soon found it made me so "unanxious" that my once active life was lost. I sat in my apartment day after day, month after month and, yes, year after year, alone and subdued to the point that my motivation was squelched. I had been on this medication for about two years and realized I was sinking more and more into a scary depression — scary because I seemed to have lost my will to fight — yet I knew I needed to bring my life back to an even keel. It was imperative that I get my doctor to listen —and he did. He trusted my judgments of my body and my meds. Though it has taken years to arrive at this place of being trusted effectively by a psychiatrist, I have. But it took being open, honest with him and persistent.

Though my surroundings are comfortable and I increasingly enjoy my own company, I still often hesitate to leave the apartment unless I am with another person. During this time on Loxapine, I did not go very far afield from my place alone — not even to the grocery store. At the recommendation of a friend, I signed up for the Sendial Program with Thrifty Foods. I placed a grocery order each week, and the groceries were delivered it to my door.

In the end my psychiatrist reduced my medication, and now I am on a very minimal dose. With the decrease, I perked up almost right away, immediately taking up walking again (up to 8,000 steps a day,) painting and going out to various destinations by myself. I was relying on my friends and family less and less to take me on errands and outings as I discovered more and more of my newfound freedom. I was alive again and wanting to do more and more things. I had returned to the "thrive model," and life began to more quickly and positively move forward, with lots of new adventures.

All my life I have been a walker. But about five years ago, after many falls, I accepted that I needed a walker. With it, I could still walk for hours if I kept to basic, repetitive paths to accommodate my agoraphobia, or at least until my legs would give out.

But in early 2016 I injured my knee while on the bus. As I started to sit down and pull my walker out of the way, my knee went the opposite direction to the rest of my body and I heard a loud crunching sound. The injury laid me up for almost 10 months because of the severe pain. It wasn't until I was able to get physio at the Victoria Arthritis Centre that my knee eased enough to allow me to walk again, though still with a walker or a cane.

Unfortunately, this injury and being homebound brought the agoraphobia back even more intensely. I found it harder and harder to climb out from under it this time, and I began to miss my freedom. I became quite isolated during this period, spending my time doing art, colouring and word-find puzzles. I did not interact with other people much, and my anxieties increased substantially as a result.

I did enrol in a depression management group at the Mental Health Centre during the summer of 2016 and stayed long enough to hone some skills in dealing with depression. But the group did not really address my anxieties. I left the group several weeks before it was to end.

Still, I have had very few depressive periods since. I now know I need to reach out and find help for myself. And I know that there is help out there. I have learned to navigate the mental health system to get the help I need.

Navigating the system takes a good case manager. Hayley, with her encouragement and support, provided me with the information on where and when and what programs would be useful for me at any one time. If I said yes, she would put in a referral for me. The experiences in each program gave me the skills to help others navigate the system as well. I could share and rate the effectiveness of the different programs, encourage them to talk with their case managers and ultimately take control of their own healing. I know about programs in the community, such as recreation centres and even the public library. People now look up to me as a mentor, and I am very happy to share my knowledge of the mazes that make up our mental health system.

Since the summer of 2017, I have been getting counselling through the Esquimalt Neighbourhood House for my "high risk" behaviour and suicidal ideations. Though the sessions have been painful and intense, all is going well. My counsellor, Faith, has been wonderfully compassionate and supportive of the healing that has come from bursts of painful crying jags and despairing energy, including a session after a very a close call of suicide. Now, instead of seeing life situations in black and white, I am seeing many of the greyer areas once again — an important coping skill. I also worked with Faith to come to terms with the impact my book was having on me, and how it would affect those reading it. Now I feel at ease with what I have to present, and with myself, and my therapy is winding down and a peaceful happiness has moved in. The counselling was the right move at the right time. I have healed so much of my memories of the past and am now feeling free enough to embrace today and my future.

As well, I am involved in a Senior's Supportive Network for people 55-plus suffering from anxiety and depression at the one of the local community mental health centres run by Island Health. This is an afternoon fun time where it is safe just to be myself. I love it and see already that this program is increasing my social skills, my ability to deal with isolation and my sense of freedom and joy. I am teaching arts and crafts to my group, and will soon start working with another group, called Bridges — a program for mentally ill adults with cognitive disabilities. I am, once again, voluntarily involved in the mental health community, something I had never dreamed I would do again.

Even though I still struggle with trying new activities, and my agoraphobia lurks in the far corners of my mind, my goal for the coming years is to be involved in more community activities around theology, art and culture; to walk in areas of town not familiar to me so that I might take in the beauty, charm and uniqueness of God's world, as well as give me more exercise; to be more able to talk to people who scare me and to form a bond with them, letting them know how frightening my interactions are with them; and to work more consistently to overcome my social fears.

My goal, in short, is to have more exposure to a different type of lifestyle — non-restrictive and life-giving — and also to open myself up to evening adventures with friends, going to movies, plays, concerts and other out-of-the-norm activities for me that take me from my 5 p.m. bedtime.

Somehow I know that I can accomplish this, as I have climbed over bigger hurdles in my lifetime. Just as I once could never imagine myself not using for more than a year, I cannot even imagine what my life will look like five years from now. I sense I will have a freer, more normal life than I have ever had. I also sense that I will have ceased hiding away in my apartment, too afraid to be in the world. My freedom will come naturally and without hesitation and fear. I will be thriving in ways that will no longer be new to me.

I want people to know that there is always a place for hope. My life, with all the twists and turns it took to arrive at this place of some contentment, mental stability, sobriety, growth and success, shows a path can be found even when you feel hopelessly lost.

I have chosen to write this story of my life as a means of encouraging those struggling with mental illness and/or addiction, and to show that life has an interesting way of evening itself out.

To reach this new pinnacle in my life, I have to thank my passion for art and my fish, and the support I have received all along from staff, my case manager, my family and friends. My art has given me a way to utilize the energy I would have put into using. My troop of family, friends and workers have given me a taste of the freedom that is happening — and, yes, is still happening.

Each day I see God moulding my life in a way I never really saw before. I am no longer a victim, but a true survivor of my own mental frailties. Destiny has taken on a new, positive meaning for me.

The staff here at Rockland tell me over and over again that I will be staying with them for quite a while because I am succeeding in this environment. I have never succeeded anywhere else before. I am chuffed at this observation, and look forward to a creative, adventurous and full life here. My kick at the can, my windy name and past, are all evolving into a life of wisdom that I can share with others. I am learning to "be" instead of "doing." I am closer to becoming whole, more than I have ever been before.

I wish all of you reading my book find this state of being. The rewards of making it this far outweigh the storms of my past. Mental illness does not have to dictate or define life. You too can be free. Letting go of being a victim and striving to thrive as a survivor will bring unexpected healing to your life. Go for the victories. Go for the Hope. Both these goals are available to you. Try to not look back, but stay in the mindful moment and enjoy each second of it. May it be so.

30 GOD'S NOT FINISHED WITH ME YET

Shortly after the passing of Pat Piddington in 1997 and the retirement of her husband Mike, who had been reverend at St. Paul's Anglican church — now St. Peter's and St. Paul's — in Esquimalt, my life took a new spiritual route.

During the last couple of years in the Lampson Street apartment my faith faced many challenges. I continued to attend St. Paul's, but after Mike retired I was not greeted with great enthusiasm. A new minister, very evangelistic, took over. He and I did not see eye to eye on many topics, particularly on being a lesbian in the Anglican Church, which then considered this contrary to scripture. Early in 1998 we had an animated, even volatile, discussion of me being a lesbian (though not a practising one). He told me I was no longer accepted in his church, and if I continued attending he would refuse to give me the Sacraments.

I was so angry at this rejection, I phoned a United Church almost on the other edge of town. I had met the minister there, also a lesbian, at a drop-in dinner group many months before, and asked if I could visit her.

I sensed the United Church was less formal about the "gay" issue, but even knowing this I arrived at the appointed time and stood sheepishly on the church's doorstep, quivering in my newly acquired scooter boots. I had started getting around town on a motor scooter many months before, giving me the freedom to easily explore other parts of Victoria. This United Church, though a long distance away from where I was living, was very much accessible by scooter, yet I was not yet comfortable with the leather jacket, heavy boots and helmet that I was wearing to show up at a new church. The new minister had a good chuckle when I admitted this clothing issue to her.

After giving me a background of the church's history, she took me on a tour of the sanctuary and the hall. Her gentleness and attentiveness helped me relax a little, and she said, with open arms, that she would look forward to me coming to her church and hopefully feeling at home there.

I arrived the following Sunday, still chagrined at my dress. Since I had first met Pat and Mike, I had never been so warmly welcomed as I was by this congregation. My inhibitions relaxed — not easily, but with great emotional discomfort. My spiritual life still felt unsettled, dangling. But about a year after I arrived at this church, I transferred my membership from the Anglican to the United Church. It was a tough decision, as I knew I was saying a firm goodbye to my childhood faith and beliefs and saying hello to a whole new spiritual life.

For many years, I struggled with the loss of the structure of the Anglican services — the kneeling and chanting in particular. This United Church seemed so very progressive, and I was still firmly planted in the need and comfort of ritual.

As the first year in my new church unfolded, I was using again. I not only felt the discomfort of a new environment, but also shame. I was sliding into depression, and did not want people to know that I was a psychiatric patient with a terrible, out-of-control substance habit.

Many years later, I realized the shame was unwarranted. This congregation had totally welcomed me, solvent smell and all.

For most of life — up until after my 60th birthday — shame about my addiction and mental illness never left me.

But then, finally, I started to gain some stability. I had more and more changes in medications and my highs became less extreme my depressions less deep. While the swings were not as big, I still had many, many within a day and week.

But no matter what state I was in, the congregation humbly accepted me and took me eagerly into their fold. Right from my first moments in that church, I believe they cared a lot about me.

After 19 years, I am still at this church, though now questioning how the new ministry upholds my spiritual needs. There are lots of changes in vision for my church, which is choosing to become a centre for spiritual growth with the hiring of a new minister. I now question whether or not this church fits my spiritual needs.

Though my spiritual life seems more grounded, my moods are still erratic. Yet even as I struggle to deal with these changes, I'm aware that I have been through enough faith challenges to know that I can rise to the spiritual honing I need in my life.

I still struggle with my spirituality. But I'm thankful for all the ministers in my past who have helped me along my life road. I probably would never have made it to this point, where much new hope and personal freedom reign, without them.

When I started my spiritual life anew at this United Church I was still angry at God, and refused to accept the human form of God, Jesus Christ. I was bitter and resented God's intrusion in my life, even though I seemed to keep on seeking him. I became aware of Sophie, the feminine side of God, and she seemed less frightening and judgmental. I had first heard of Sophie at St. John's Church, as the Anglican Church struggled with the idea of God being both male and female.

I found her comforting and caring. This discovery brought the beginning of peace to my spiritual life. I could talk to Sophie (actually known as Sophia, but I prefer to call the female side of God Sophie) in a very natural way, and the volatile, combative interactions with God the Father ceased. No longer would I pray to HIM. She was my salvation. Of course, as the years went by, God the Father became present to me in other forms: God the Creator, the Redeemer, the Healer, the Everlasting, the Protector. I continued on, though, talking with Sophie and accepting her guidance for my life. The punitive faith struggle seemed to be drawing to an end. Also I was beginning to accept Jesus, who I had more than ignored up until this point, into my life. First with great hesitation, and then with much more certainty. Yes, my spiritual life has become stronger and much more a part of my life.

Not being in conflict about my faith became a more natural way of life. I could finally accept that: 1) I was being cared for in the utmost, universal way — with love; 2) I was forgiven for my rage against the Creator; 3) I was laying down my sword and stepping back from the faith battle and finding much comfort in my new journey with God; and 4) I was happier about my spiritual prospects than I had ever been before. I had a new lease on life, including prayer and many, many candid and frank talks with God Sophie every day.

I still felt so very uncomfortable about my sexuality, yet I was glad to be worshipping in a sanctuary in which this lifestyle, and all lifestyles that were not violent or invasive of other people's rights, were acceptable. The minister and her partner befriended me, much in the same way Pat had years earlier.

Still, my first years in this church were not easy. My relationship with the minister and her partner was complicated by my growing mood swings, addiction and suicidal feelings. I pestered both her and her partner for support and companionship. What had been a positive experience turned sour as I pushed all the buttons of the minister, making her, in the end, so sick physically that she had to leave the church. One night she just collapsed at home, in great physical pain. She was, I suppose, exhausted with all the responsibilities that she had taken on at the church, and, perhaps with me. Finally, she had to turn to her bed and solitude to heal. She was in tremendous emotional pain and had to step back from her ministry for a while. When she did return, the dynamics of her position had changed. Ultimately, she resigned. Though I couldn't take all the responsibility for her illness, I felt I needed to take a huge chunk.

Her partner also drifted away from me, though we had spent many hours together travelling back and forth to the North Shore in Vancouver to see a diet doctor. We had long, long conversations and, in fact, I knew her better than my minister. When they left our church, I was devastated and guilt-ridden.

Yet, further down in my spiritual core, I felt a bit of hope lurking. I fought against this hope for another few years because I still felt I did not deserve to live, but eventually the will to live became stronger and stronger. My faith became much more outward than inward; I could begin to see the needs of others and not just myself. I could tithe my money so that I was able to support, at first, the church coffers. Later I was able to give money to a few other community programs that helped other people — the homeless, the sexually abused, people in other nations. For the first time in my Christian life, I felt that I was giving back to the world and God, and I could say "Thanks, God, for being with me all these years. I do not know what your purpose for me is, but heck, you have kept me alive all this time, when in fact I should have been dead decades ago." I suspected there really was a purpose for me.

As I write this in 2017, I realize that perhaps one reason Sophie and

God the Father, Creator, Healer have kept me alive is to give hope to other people struggling with mental illness, addiction and other related issues. It took me years to discover this gem of a feeling, and now I want to pass it along to others. Faith kept me alive even though I fought it all the way. My journey in finding peace was a very rocky one, like Moses wandering in the desert for 40 years looking for the promised land. My journey took almost 66 years, but I found my own Israel within.

I still have mood swings and suicidal thoughts, but my life is based on hope and caring now. I have developed an ability to listen to people early in their journeys. Like God did for me, I strive to listen without offering advice — though sometimes the need to give advice is irresistible. I feel I have a lot of wisdom to offer, and a lot of things to learn.

God certainly has not finished with me yet. My journey is just beginning — a new bend in the road, an untravelled path that will take me to wherever I am meant to go. I now have long dialogues with Sophie and even the male side of God, and these talks seem so natural. My character flaws are many, to be sure, but the positive aspects of my life outweigh my human frailties. I will always have a mental illness and will always struggle with the niggles of addiction, yet now I can stand up in the presence of God and be counted as one of his faithful. I am blessed.

As far as my sexuality goes, I am now becoming more open with my bodily choices and making lesbian friends at church. My shame is not as deep as when I first entered this congregation. And I have been given hope that one day I can eradicate these feelings.

In the end, I've discovered, God is at the beginning and the end. Perhaps I take my mortality for granted now. But I marvel with unceasing wonder at how all the acts of violence I did to myself have left me a brain that shows no signs of damage, a heart that beats strong, a set of lungs clear and undamaged and a wisdom that came from somewhere. I am one of God's miracles… I entrust to Him and to Her my life for the rest of my time.

ACKNOWLEDGEMENTS

I have been supported by many caring, gentle friends who stayed with me when life was rough and were there to celebrate when the tough times lifted. They continued to walk with me throughout my huffing years, my years of suicide attempts and hospitalizations, and my years of mood swings.

I wish to acknowledge these friends, as I have no other way to thank them for their love and devotion.

Joan Smith and Claudia Dorrington were my first non-judgmental, caring, no-strings-attached friends, and are still friends today. Jody P. went to bat for me when my chips were down. I am ever grateful to the three of them for their faith in me and their friendships.

Later on, when I joined the United Church, I gained many new and wonderful friends, including Ann M., Susan G., Barbara H., and the Fyles — Shirley and Jim (both now deceased.) Dr. C was added to my palette a few years later. She was not part of my church life, but became an integral part of my daily life. I could not ask for better friends along with Joan and Claudia and then Jody P., who came much later.

Originally I met Ann M. at the United Church I was attending, and she has taken me out almost every weekend since then for the last 18 years. Conversation is not always necessary anymore; we can communicate with silence. We have had ups and downs but we share the deep love of music and the outdoors — especially Butchart Gardens. We also share our faith. She met me the evening after the curtain was dropped on a musical, Noyes Fludd, put on by my church in 2000. I had a small part and sang in the choir. The last night of the musical I fell into a sniffing heap, plagued by anger, fear, voices and unpleasant visions. Ann was called from a lecture at a nearby church by another friend of mine to come to my aid. I was in mental agony when Ann arrived at my place. After a few hours she left, but later that night I phoned her, and Ann and her husband came and picked me up and took me to their home for the rest of the night. By morning, embarrassed beyond words, I asked to be taken home. Ann and I became close friends after that. She has been so generous and giving. My gratitude will never be enough to say "Thanks."

When I joined the United Church, I was still an avid singer. I joined the folk choir and met Susan G. there. Though I was so very shy and almost afraid to open my mouth to sing, I stood in front of the congregation with Susan at my side — she often playing the tambourine — and sang rousingly, loudly and with great energy and enthusiasm. Over the years Susan has been a generous friend, coming over to my place weekly for a short visit and a chat. For many years she spoke to me on the telephone every morning as I struggled with the emotions of my life. She has fought cancer and won. I admire her courage and her strong will. Again, I have been blessed.

Barbara H. had joined the same United Church around the time I did. Eventually, when she was interested in becoming a lay or a diaconal minister, I sat on her discernment committee, which was part of the process. Our friendship became very close as a result. I challenged her in these meetings and she rose to the challenges as she struggled through five years of studies. Barbara is my age, and she went back to college to become a diaconal minister. My admiration for her grew as she wrestled with the disadvantages (and advantages) of being a mature student with dyslexia, finally graduating in 2014. She asked me to be part of her Coveting Service — an ordination-type service that gave her authority to carry out her ministry in the church — and I humbly said "Yes." We speak on the phone quite often on Saturday morning. She has a special knack to buoy me up when I am down. Our lives have become intermingled and I have become part of her family. She always has me over on Christmas morning for stockings with the rest of her crew. I so appreciate her affections and her joyous, energetic presence. And her washer and dryer know me well — I often do my laundry at her place.

The Fyles — Jim and Shirley — were an older couple whose charm and love put people at ease. Their Sunday after-church "toasted cheese sandwiches" always hit the spot, as did the visits that happened around their cluttered kitchen table. Early on I considered them my grandparents and was delighted one Easter, when I was estranged from my family, to have an Easter egg hunt all to myself in their sprawling backyard at the base of Mount Tolmie. The Fyles took me on impromptu picnics to Cattle Point and walked with me when I was in a turmoil about my sexuality. They were key figures in the Victoria chapter of PFLAG — Parents and Friends of Lesbians and Gays — and I used their knowledge to help me come to terms, somewhat, with my sexuality. Shirley and I would walk up Mount Tolmie as I poured out my heart and she listened intently without offering advice. Jim would always be back home making tea for our return. They passed away quite recently and I miss them so, so much. They were grandparents for sure — especially when we sat across the table from each other in McDonald's eating filet of fish and fries topped off with a strawberry shake. I adored them and I miss them, yet somehow I know they are still walking with me because I hear their special chuckle now and again when I am puzzled or sad.

Norma K. graduated a couple of years ahead of me from Victoria High School and we had been friends when Betty and I lived on Gladstone Street. She and her husband Rod would come to some of our costume parties — I remember the two of them sitting on the narrow floor of our kitchen eating out of those silly tin cans on Hobo Night. Norma went into nursing, and I met up with her again during my many admissions to the Eric Martin Pavilion, where she worked in the psychiatric intensive care ward. Even though we were on different sides of the psychological fence, we really never lost touch after that. Every Christmas she would send me a Christmas card with a bit of news on her family's adventures. Eventually, when they moved to Metchosin and she stopped working at Eric Martin, our friendship took off again. Like Susan G., Norma kept in touch daily for many, many years. She has listened to hours and hours of my tormented stories, and of my victorious ones. She has encouraged me to temper my activities to avoid the highs and lows due to the bipolar disorder. Even when I always seemed to fall into the highs or lows, she was there to listen without judgment. Norma has been a gem with a great sense of humour and a relaxed voice. We live far away from each other, but we are close souls that no distance can tear away.

And finally, I want to introduce you to Dr. C. Since my hospitalization in 2001 after the suicide attempt, Dr. C. was my general practitioner. The other GP I had scared the pants off me, and was always telling me to lose weight. Finally, I went on a huge solvent binge and stopped eating until I was down to about 104 pounds from over 180, leaving me looking like a famine victim. I never seemed to be able to please this doctor.

Then Dr. C. came along. I met her when I was in the EMP during that turbulent year. She was the doctor of my friend Beth, and I got to know her during visits. When I was discharged from the hospital I asked Dr. C. if she would be my doctor. I was given a six-month trial. After six months, when I asked, anxiously, if I had passed, she said yes. Up until she retired around 2012 she remained my doctor. I was using heavily for much of that time, and her education as a drug and alcohol counsellor came in handy. I was also afraid of her. Often I would drag a friend to my appointments because I was afraid of stirring up her ire at my obvious using. She seemed to take it all in stride. When I was living at Rockland — after she retired — her house was nearby and we would have tea, at her house or mine. We maintain somewhat of a professional relationship, but enjoy each other's company. I am blessed to have had her as my GP, and now even more blessed to have her as my friend.

There are many other people who have befriended me over the years and stuck with me — just too many to list.

To all my friends, I say "Thank you" for sticking with me all these tumultuous years. I could never have made the progress I have without any one of you. I am truly blessed.

I also want to offer thanks to four non-profit organizations. I have been helped by many agencies over the years, but this book would not have been possible without the compassionate, loving kindness and dedication of the people that served me at these organizations.

The Victoria Sexual Assault Centre provided me with exceptional and extensive counselling around my childhood abuse — not just the sexual abuse, but all the other abuse as well. The counsellor I had, Barb, provided the necessary grounding to work through the secrets and dissociative behaviours I had struggled with so long. The 18 months of counselling didn't produce immediate change, but in time it helped me to become more successful in my life's journey. Barb's departure brought another crisis, as I had fallen deeply in love with her. I plagued the centre's crisis line counsellor for more than two years with sobbing, hysterical calls about this loss. As a result, I was granted another six months of counselling by the centre. I misused the time. I returned to the comforts of my addiction and missed many appointments because of intoxication, and was finally discharged after many missed appointments. My new counsellor scared me, because her first words to me were: "Don't you dare fall in love with me." Though I had not intended to fall in love twice, I was deterred by her bluntness. I realize now that I just could not handle any more time with the centre because my pain was so deep, and I felt I would not receive any empathy from this worker. I shamed myself with the way I handled the last few months of counselling, and expect the VSAC was unhappy with me. In spite of my bad behaviour, I grew as a result of my involvement with the centre and was eventually able to live my life in relative peace. I did not deserve all the time they allotted me, but I am ever so thankful for their thoroughness.

The second organization is The Victoria Hospice. As Pat was dying, and after she had gone, I was given counselling to help me work through my intense grief. Later, when a loved great-aunt in Winnipeg died, I returned to hospice for more counselling. For most of my life I had been unable to deal with grief and death except by getting intoxicated and skipping the funerals. Hospice let me share my losses and become less frightened when facing death. I was at peace, finally, and was able to also put aside regret about the funerals of friends and family that I had missed over the years. These days I am able to visit people as they are slipping away and attend their Celebrations of Life. Death is no longer a last hurrah for me, but a way for love to be released into the universe where it will be with me forever.

The Umbrella Society, a group of counsellors who were addicts themselves at one point, journeyed with me through withdrawal, slips and the frightening drug and alcohol system. Kiran, my worker at the Umbrella Society, helped me get into detox on a couple of occasions — only to have them ban me because of behaviours related to my mental health issues.

Through her support and caring I was eventually able to be sober. I had never had anyone in my life to actually walk with me, on a sometimes daily basis, in my efforts to shake my addiction. Kiran, you believed in me, even when I did not.

And finally, the Esquimalt Neighbourhood House. I was introduced to the neighbourhood house during a practicum placement with the Laurel Enterprise program, with the idea I would volunteer there. I enjoyed the atmosphere and the staff so much that I did, in fact, volunteer there after my practicum for about three or four years under Sandy Whalley. The neighbourhood house played a huge role in my life during the 1990s to 2001 and, often was my only contact with concerned professional people during my tormented time around the years 2000 and 2001.

They continually sought help for me from the psychiatric and alcohol and drug systems but, to their frustration, I am sure, never received it. Brenda Macevicius and Kris Klusmier kept in constant touch with me, making sure I was safe during 2000 right up to a suicide attempt in 2001. Without their help I probably wouldn't have survived this attempt.

During 2017 and 2018 they provided me with top-notch counselling that extended far beyond the usual ten-week maximum. For ten months with one of their members of the counselling centre training program, Faith, offered me free and intense counselling support. This support has changed the focus of my life tremendously and without it, I would still be at home, totally depressed and not contributing to the world around me. Faith's work with me has liberated me so much so that my world is full of new options and techniques to deal with suicidal thinking. My gratitude for Faith's help and the help of Esquimalt Neighbourhood House goes beyond any boundaries that my limited mind can contain.

Thank you so, so much. You all have changed my life's journey and opened up my potential to give back.

To all of you, the Victoria Sexual Assault Centre, Victoria Hospice the Umbrella Society and Esquimalt Neighbourhood House, thanks.

ABOUT THE AUTHOR

Gayle Chapman is well known in the Victoria mental health system as a "tough nut to crack." Despite a life in and out of psychiatric hospitals from her teens to her 60s — or perhaps because of it — she created a successful program partnering people with mental illness and volunteers, and was honoured as volunteer of the year by the B.C. Division of Canadian Mental Health and nominated for a Women of Distinction Award. She's an accomplished artist and survivor. This is her first book.

Manufactured by Amazon.ca
Bolton, ON